Crocheting Tablecloths and Placemats

Crocheting Tablecloths and Placemats

Edited by Florence Weinstein

Dover Publications, Inc., New York

Published in Canada by General Publishing Company, Ltd., 30 Lesmill Road, Don Mills, Toronto,
Ontario.
Published in the United Kingdom by Constable
and Company, Ltd., 10 Orange Street, London WC 2.

This Dover edition, first published in 1975, is an
unabridged republication of *Crochet for Tables,*
published in 1943 by the Spool Cotton Company;
Tables of Tomorrow, published in 1939 by The
Spool Cotton Company; *New Table Talk,* published
in 1941 by The Spool Cotton Company; *New Table
Settings,* published in 1937 by The Spool Cotton
Company; and *Tablecloth Book,* published in 1944
by The American Thread Company. This edition
also contains a new introduction by the editor.

International Standard Book Number: 0-486-20659-9
Library of Congress Catalog Card Number: 74-21221

Manufactured in the United States of America
Dover Publications, Inc.
180 Varick Street
New York, N.Y. 10014

Introduction

This is a collection of some of the most beautiful crocheted lace patterns published in magazines and brochures thirty years ago. Hand crocheted table linen was extremely popular during this period and then went out of fashion. Today with the increase of leisure time, we are returning to the joy of creating all sorts of handmade articles, and the crocheting of lace is enjoying a new surge of popularity.

The laundering of a crocheted tablecloth used to be a very difficult procedure. By using some of the new synthetic threads now on the market, we can make the washing and drying of a lace tablecloth much less of the time-consuming project it used to be. Although many of the threads suggested are still available, I would recommend the use of our new cottons, synthetics and polyesters. Whatever type of thread you decide to use, be sure to buy at one time sufficient thread of the same dye lot to complete the article you wish to make. It is impossible to avoid slight variations in color in different dye lots.

Since most of the cloths in this book are made by crocheting small motifs and then joining these motifs together until the desired size is obtained, the component parts can be used to make a wide variety of other objects such as ponchos, scarves, purses, mantillas, etc.

The needle sizes and gauges suggested in the directions are still in use today. Before starting any article, make a small test sample of the stitch or motif. If your working tension is too loose or too tight, use a finer or coarser needle to obtain the correct gauge.

FLORENCE WEINSTEIN

Brooklyn, New York
November, 1974

CROCHET STITCHES

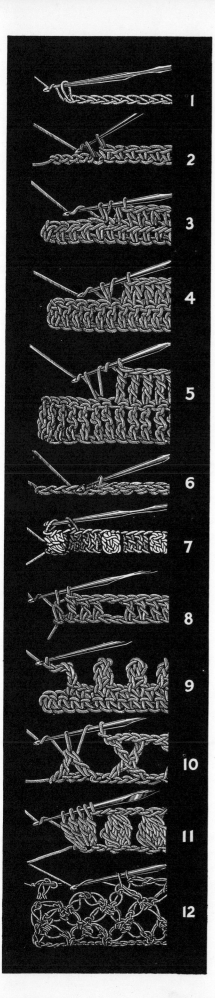

1 ... Chain (ch): Make loop in thread, insert hook in loop, and draw main length of thread through. Continue to draw thread through each new loop formed for length desired.

2 ... Single Crochet (s c): Insert hook under 2 loops of st, draw thread through st (2 loops on hook), thread over hook, draw through the 2 loops.

3 ... Half Double Crochet (half d c): Make like d c until there are 3 loops on hook; then thread over and draw through all 3 loops.

4 ... Double Crochet (d c): Thread over hook, insert hook in st, and draw thread through (3 loops on hook), thread over hook, draw through 2 loops, thread over, draw through 2 remaining loops.

5 ... Treble (tr): Thread over hook twice, insert hook in st and draw thread through st (4 loops on hook), thread over, draw through 2 loops, thread over, draw through 2 loops, thread over, draw through remaining 2 loops. For a **Double Treble (d tr)**, thread over hook 3 times; and for a **Triple Treble (tr tr)**, thread over hook 4 times, taking off 2 loops at a time as in the tr.

6 ... Slip Stitch (sl st): Insert hook through st, catch thread and, with one motion, draw through both the st and the 1 loop on hook. The sl st is used for joining, or when an invisible st is required.

7 ... Popcorn Stitch (pc st): Ch 1, 5 d c in next st, drop st from hook, insert hook back in ch-1 and draw loop through the one on hook.

8 ... Block (bl) and Space (sp): Make 4 d c over 4 sts of preceding row (this forms 1 bl), ch 2, skip 2 sts, make 1 sp. The bl and sp are used in Filet Crochet.

9 ... Picot (p): Make a ch of 3, 4, or 5 sts, according to length of p desired, and s c in the foundation, or in 1st st of ch.

10 ... Cross Stitch: Thread over twice, insert hook in st and draw thread through as for a tr (4 loops on hook), thread over, and draw through 2 loops, thread over, skip 2 sts, insert hook in next st, draw thread through (5 loops on hook), thread over and draw off 2 loops at a time 4 times, ch 2, 1 d c in the center point of the cross, thus completing the cross.

11 ... Cluster: Make 3 or more tr in the same st, always holding the last loop of each tr on the hook; then, thread over hook and take off all remaining loops. Then make a tight ch to fasten the cluster.

12 ... Knot Stitch: Draw a loop on hook out ¼ inch, draw thread through, making a ch st of it. Put hook between loop and single thread of this ch and make an s c. Work another similar knot st, skip 4 sts of preceding row, 1 s c in next. Repeat from beginning to end of row. Make two ⅜-inch knot sts to turn, 1 s c over double loop at right of 1st center knot of preceding row, 1 s c over double loop at left of same knot, 2 knot sts and repeat.

ABBREVIATIONS FOR CROCHET

Chain	ch	Triple Treble	tr tr	Picot	p
Single Crochet	s c	Slip Stitch	sl st	Stitch	st
Half Double Crochet	half d c	Popcorn Stitch	pc st	Round	rnd
Double Crochet	d c	Block	bl	Inclusive	incl.
Treble	tr	Space	sp	Increase	inc.
Double Treble	d tr			Decrease	dec.

* (asterisk) ... When this symbol appears, continue working until instructions refer you back to this symbol.

Crocheting Tablecloths and Placemats

January

Here's a pattern that's simple as "Happy New Year." Make a Buffet Cloth as shown or a full table size. The small motif goes very quickly.

January

Materials Required—AMERICAN THREAD COMPANY
"STAR" or "GEM" MERCERIZED CROCHET
COTTON. Size 20—White, Cream or Ecru.

10—250 Yd. Balls will make a scarf 20 x 50 inches.

Each Motif Measures about 1¾ inches.

372 Motifs (12 x 31) are required for scarf illustrated.

Steel Crochet Hook No. 11 or 12.

MOTIF. Ch 10, join, ch 1 and work 16 s c into ring, join.

2nd Row. Ch 5, d c in next s c, * ch 2, d c in next s c, repeat from * all around, ch 2. Join in 3rd st of ch 5 (16 meshes).

3rd Row. Ch 1 and work 3 s c in each mesh, join.

4th Row. Ch 7, d c between groups of s c (over d c of 2nd row) * ch 4, d c between next 2 groups of s c, repeat from * all around, ch 4, join in 3rd st of ch 7 (16 meshes).

5th Row. Ch 5, skip 1 mesh, 3 tr c in next mesh, ch 5, 3 tr c in same mesh, ch 5, skip 1 mesh, sl st in next d c, ch 7, sl st in next d c, repeat from beginning 3 times, join, break thread.

To join motifs, work a shell and 7 ch loop, ch 5, 3 tr c in next loop, ch 3, sl st in center st of ch 5 of 1st motif, ch 3, complete shell of 2nd motif, ch 5, skip 1 mesh, sl st in next d c, ch 3, sl st in center st of ch 7 of 1st motif, ch 3, s c in next d c, ch 5 and work a shell joining it to 1st motif same as last shell. Complete motif and join all motifs in same manner.

EDGE. Starting at corner, ch 5, d c in same space, ch 2, d c in same space, ch 2, d c in same space, ch 4, sl st in top of d c for picot, * ch 2, d c in same space, repeat from * twice, ** ch 5, s c in next loop, ch 5, 2 d c in next loop, ch 4, sl st in top of d c for picot, d c in same space, ch 5, s c in next loop, ch 5, d c between joining of motifs, ch 2, d c in same space, ch 2, d c in same space, ch 4, sl st in top of d c for picot, ch 2, d c in same space, ch 2, d c in same space, repeat from ** all around, working each corner same as 1st corner.

To Make Napkins to use with scarf, cut squares of linen the size required. Over a narrow hem work a row of s c and finish with edge same as scarf.

Work one motif finished with a row of s c for each napkin. Insert into corner of napkin and cut out linen under motif if desired.

February

This cloth has the flavor of Lincoln's time. Decorate with a miniature log cabin and a few snowy evergreens

Materials Required—AMERICAN THREAD COMPANY "STAR" or "GEM" MERCERIZED CROCHET COTTON, Size 20 White, Cream or Ecru

63—250 Yd. Balls are required for Cloth illustrated.

Steel Crochet Hook No. 10 or 11.

Each large motif measures about 7 inches. Cloth 8 x 11 motifs will measure about 56 x 77 inches.

MOTIF. Ch 10, join to form a ring, ch 3, 2 d c in ring, ch 4, sl st in last d c for picot, * 3 d c, picot, repeat from * 6 times, sl st in 1st ch 3 to join, sl st in next d c.

2nd Row. Ch 10, 1 d c between next 2 picots, * ch 7, 1 d c between next 2 picots, repeat from * 5 times, ch 7, sl st in 3rd st of ch 10.

3rd Row. Over each loop work 1 s c, ch 1, 4 d c, picot, 4 d c, ch 1, 1 s c, join and break thread. Work 7 more motifs joining them at 2 picots on each side leaving 1 petal of each motif free on inside of circle and 3 petals on the outside of circle. (To join, ch 2, sl st in picot of previous motif, ch 2, sl st back in last d c to complete picot.)

CENTER MOTIF. Work a motif, sl st to 2nd d c of 1st petal, (ch 3 counts as 1 d c) * ch 6, s c in 5th st from hook for picot, ch 3, join with a sl st to picot of free petal on one motif, ch 8, sl st in 5th st from hook for picot, ch 1, skip both picots, 1 tr c in next st of ch that counts as a d c, skip picot on petal, 1 d c in next d c, ch 9, sl st in 5th st from hook for picot, ch 6, sl st in 5th st from hook for picot, ch 3 and fasten to joining picots of motifs, ch 8, sl st in 5th st from hook for picot, ch 1, 1 s c between previous pair of picots, ch 5 for picot, skip next picot, 2 s c over next ch, ch 3, 1 d c in 2nd d c of next petal, repeat from * all around ending row with ch 3, sl st in 3rd st of 1st ch, break thread.

BORDER. Join thread to 2nd d c of center petal of one motif, ch 3 for a d c, * ch 7, skip picot, 1 d c in next 3 d c, ch 4, 1 d c in 2nd d c of next petal, ch 8, skip picot, 1 d tr c in next 3rd d c, ch 3, 1 d tr c in 2nd d c of first petal on next motif, ch 8, skip picot, 1 d c in next 3rd d c,

ch 4, 1 d c in 2nd d c of next petal, repeat from * all around joining in 3rd st of ch 10.

2nd Row. Ch 3, * 3 d c in next 7 ch loop, 3 d c in 4th st of same loop, 3 d c over remainder of same loop, 1 d c in d c, 4 d c in 4 ch loop, d c in d c, 8 d c over next loop, d c in tr c, 3 d c over next loop, d c in tr c, 8 d c over next loop, d c in d c, 4 d c over next loop, d c in d c, repeat from * all around, join.

3rd Row. Ch 3 and work 1 d c in each d c at sides and 3 d c in each center st of corners.

JOINING MOTIF. Ch 8, join, ch 3, 23 d c in ring, join.

2nd Row. Ch 3, d c in same space, ch 3, 2 d c in same space, * ch 5, skip 2 d c, s c in next st, ch 5, skip 2 d c, 2 d c, ch 3, 2 d c in next st, repeat from * twice, ch 5, skip 2 d c, s c in next st, ch 5, join in 3rd st of ch.

3rd Row. Sl st into 3 ch loop, ch 3, d c in same loop, ch 3, 2 d c in same loop, * ch 3, 2 d c in next loop, ch 5, 2 d c in next loop, ch 3, shell in shell, repeat from * twice, ch 3, 2 d c in next loop, ch 5, 2 d c in next loop, ch 3, join in 3rd st of ch.

4th Row. Sl st into loop, * shell in shell, ch 3, 2 d c in next loop, ch 5, s c in center st of next loop, ch 5, 2 d c in next loop, ch 3, repeat from * all around, join.

5th Row. Sl st into loop, * shell in shell, ch 3, 2 d c in next loop, ch 3, 2 d c in next loop, ch 5, 2 d c in next loop, ch 3, 2 d c in next loop, ch 3, repeat from * all around, join.

6th Row. Sl st into loop, * shell in shell, ch 3, 2 d c in next loop, ch 3, 2 d c in next loop, ch 5, s c in center st of next loop, ch 5, 2 d c in next loop, ch 3, 2 d c in next loop, ch 3, repeat from * all around, join.

7th Row. Sl st into loop, 4 d c, ch 3, 4 d c in same loop, * ch 1, 4 d c in next loop, repeat from * 5 times, ch 1, 4 d c, ch 3, 4 d c in corner loop, repeat all around, break thread.

EDGE. Attach thread and work 1 s c in each of the next 5 s c, ch 4, sl st in 1st ch for picot, 1 s c in each of the next 5 sts and repeat all around.

March

A three-leaf Clover design (in Irish Crochet of course). Make it in white preferably; it looks so well on dark Mahogany

Materials Required—AMERICAN THREAD COMPANY "STAR" or "GEM" MERCERIZED CROCHET COTTON, Size 20

32—250 Yd. Balls White or Colors.

Steel Crochet Hook No. 11 or 12.

Each Motif measures about 3 inches. Cloth 17 x 24 motifs measures about 52 x 72 inches.

SQUARE MOTIF. Ch 6, 6 tr c in 6th st from hook, ch 1, turn, 1 s c in each tr c, ch 6, turn, 1 tr c in each s c holding the last loop of each tr c on hook, thread over, pull through 2 loops, thread over and pull through all loops on needle (cluster st), * ch 5, s c in 5th st from hook for a picot, ch 6, turn, 6 tr c in 6th st from hook, ch 1, turn, 1 s c in each tr c, ch 7, sl st in end of s c row on side of previous oval, ch 1, turn and over the ch 7, work 2 s c, ch 5, sl st in last s c for picot, 2 s c, p, 2 s c, p, 2 s c, sl st in next s c, ch 6, tr c in same s c, 1 tr c in each of the next 5 s c working all 6 tr c into a cluster st same as previous oval. Ch 5, s c in 5th st from hook for a picot, ch 6, turn, 5 tr c in 6th st from hook, ch 1, turn, 1 s c in each tr c, ch 7, sl st in side of previous oval, ch 1, turn, and over ch 7 work 2 s c, p, 2 s c, p, 2 s c, p, 2 s c, sl st in next s c, ch 6, 1 tr c in same s c, 1 tr c in each of the next 5 s c worked into a 5 tr c cluster st, ch 5, sl st in cluster st for a picot, ch 6, s c in center side of this oval, ch 5, sl st in base of oval, ** ch 6, 6 tr c in 6th st from hook, ch 1, turn, 1 s c in each tr c, ch 7, sl st in side of last oval, ch 1, turn and over ch 7 work 2 s c, p, 2 s c, p, 2 s c, p, 2 s c, sl st in next s c, ch 6, tr c in same s c and tr c in each s c worked into a cluster st, repeat from * twice and from * to **. Join work with a sl st in starting st, sl st up to center side of 1st oval,

ch 7, turn, sl st in center side of last oval, ch 1, turn and over ch 7 work 2 s c, p, 2 s c, p, 2 s c, p, 2 s c, fasten thread.

CENTER OF MOTIF. Ch 8, sl st in 5th st from hook for picot, ch 3, join with a sl st to center picot of one loop of motif, ch 7, sl st in 4th st from hook for picot, ch 3, sl st in starting point, * ch 7, sl st in 4th st from hook for picot, ch 3, sl st in center p of next loop, ch 7, sl st in 4th st from hook for picot, ch 3, sl st in starting point, repeat from * twice.

PICOT MOTIF. Join motifs by picots at each corner. Ch 10, join, ch 1 and work 16 s c into ring, sl st in 1st s c to join.

2nd Row. * Ch 6, s c in next s c, repeat from * 14 times, ch 3, d c in next s c.

3rd Row. * Ch 8, skip 1 loop, s c in next loop, repeat from * 6 times, ch 4, skip 1 loop, d c in next loop.

4th Row. ** Ch 11, s c in 5th st from hook for picot, * ch 6, p, repeat from * twice, ch 5, sl st in joining of motifs, ch 4, skip last 4 sts of ch 5, s c in next st, * ch 5, p, s c in ch 1 between next 2 picots, repeat from * twice, ch 5, p, skip next p, s c in next ch st, ch 5, s c in next 8 ch loop, ch 11, p, ch 6, p, ch 4, sl st in p on center side of square motif, ch 3, skip last 3 sts of ch 4, s c in next st, * ch 5, p, skip next p, s c in next ch st, repeat from *, ch 5, s c in next 8 ch loop and repeat from ** 3 times.

EDGE. Join at corner, * ch 6, sl st in 4th st from hook for picot, repeat from * twice, ch 2, skip 1 picot on cloth, s c in next picot, 3 picot loop, ch 2, d c in picot between the 2 ovals on cloth, 3 picot loop, ch 2, skip 1 picot, s c in next picot, 3 picot loop, ch 2, s c in top of next oval, 6 picot loop, ch 2, s c in center picot loop of next motif, 6 picot loop, ch 2, s c in top of next oval of next motif and continue all around in same manner.

April

Another simple design — with all the freshness of an Easter morning

Materials Required—AMERICAN THREAD COMPANY "STAR" or "GEM" MERCERIZED CROCHET COTTON, Size 30

29—325 Yd. Balls, White or Colors.
Steel Crochet Hook No. 11 or 12.
Each motif measures about 2¼ inches.
540 Motifs 18 x 30 are required for cloth 45 x 75.

MOTIF. Ch 10, join to form a ring, ch 4, tr c into ring, ch 4, sl st in top of tr c for picot, * 2 tr c, ch 4, sl st in top of last tr c for picot, repeat from * 10 times, join.

2nd Row. Ch 7, sl st between next 2 picots of previous row, repeat from beginning all around.

3rd Row. Sl st to center of loop, ch 6, d c in same space, * ch 5, d c in next loop, ch 3, d c in same loop, repeat from * all around, ch 5, join in 3rd st of ch 6.

4th Row. Ch 7, tr c into loop, ch 3, tr c in same loop, ch 3, tr c in same loop, ** ch 5, d c in next 3 ch loop, ch 3, d c in same loop, ch 5, d c in next 3 ch loop, ch 3, d c in same loop, ch 5, tr c in next 3 ch loop, * ch 3, tr c in same loop, repeat from * twice and repeat from ** all around joining row in 4th st of ch 7.

5th Row. Ch 3, 2 d c in next loop, 3 tr c in corner loop, ch 5, 3 tr c in same loop, 3 d c in next loop, * ch 3, 2 d c in next 3 ch loop, ch 3, 2 d c in same loop, ch 3, 2 d c, ch 3, 2 d c in next 3 ch loop, ch 3, 3 d c in next 3 ch loop, 3 tr c in next loop, ch 5, 3 tr c in same loop, 3 d c in next loop and repeat from * all around.

MOTIFS are joined together at corner chains and the chains in the 2 shells at sides of motif.

Scallop. Starting at corner, ch 9, sl st in 4th st from hook for picot, ch 1, tr c in same space, * ch 5, sl st in 4th st from hook for picot, ch 1, tr c in same space, repeat from * 3 times, ch 6, skip 5 sts, s c in next st, ** ch 4, skip loop and 2 d c, 4 tr c with (ch 1, picot, ch 1,) between each tr c in next loop, ch 4, s c in next loop, ch 4, 4 tr c with (ch 1, p, ch 1) between each tr c in next loop, ch 4, s c in 2nd st of next group, ch 6, 4 tr c with (ch 1, picot, ch 1) between each tr c in joining of next 2 motifs, ch 6, skip 5 sts of group, s c in next st, repeat from ** all around working corners same as 1st corner.

If napkins to match are desired. Cut squares of linen any size required. Over a rolled hem work a row of s c and then repeat the scallop used on cloth.

Work the 1st 3 rows of motif, finish with a row of s c and insert motif into one corner of napkin. Cut out linen under motif if desired.

9

May

Shower the June Bride in May. This cloth would make a lovely gift

Materials Required—AMERICAN THREAD COMPANY "STAR" or "GEM" MERCERIZED CROCHET COTTON, Size 30

31—325 Yd. Balls White, Cream, Ecru or Dark Linen.
Large Motif measures about 2¾ inches.
621 Motifs 23 x 27 are required for cloth 62 x 80.
Steel Crochet Hook No. 12 or 13.

LARGE MOTIF. Ch 8, join to form a ring.

1st Row. Ch 5, d c in ring, * ch 2, d c in ring, repeat from * 5 times, ch 2, join in 3rd st of ch 5 (8 spaces).

2nd Row. Sl st into space, ch 3, 2 d c in same space, * ch 3, 3 d c in next space, repeat from * all around, ch 3, join.

3rd Row. Sl st in next d c, * ch 10, s c in center d c of next group, repeat from * 6 more times, ch 3, d tr c, (3 times over needle) in base of 1st ch.

4th Row. Ch 3, 2 d c in same space, ch 4, 3 d c in same space, * ch 3, (3 d c, ch 4, 3 d c) in next loop, repeat from * all around, ch 3, join.

5th Row. Sl st to center of shell, ch 5, * 1 tr c in same space, ch 1, repeat from * 6 times, * ch 1, s c in next 3 ch loop, ch 1, 8 tr c with ch 1 between each tr c in center of next shell, repeat from * all around, ch 1, s c in next 3 ch loop, ch 1, join in 4th st of ch 5.

6th Row. * Ch 8, skip 4 tr c, s c in center space of scallop, ch 6, s c in s c just made, ch 6, s c in last s c made, ch 6, s c in last s c, s c in same space as 1st s c, ch 8, s c in s c between scallops, repeat from * all around, join, break thread.

Work another motif joining it to 1st motif in last row as follows, ch 8, skip 4 tr c, s c in center space of scallop, ch 6, s c in s c just made, ch 3, join to corresponding picot of 1st motif, ch 3, s c in last s c made, ch 6, s c in last s c, s c in same space as 1st s c and finish row same as 1st motif.

Work a 3rd motif joining it in same manner and leaving 1 scallop free for small joining.

Join 4th motif to 1st and 3rd motif in same manner.

SMALL JOINING MOTIF. Work first and second rows of large motif.

Next Row. Sl st in next d c, * ch 4, join to center picot of free scallop of large motif, ch 4, s c in center st of next group of d c of small motif, ch 12, sl st in 5th st from hook for picot, ch 7, sl st between joinings of large motif, ch 7, sl st in picot, ch 5, sl st in 1st ch for picot, ch 7, s c in center st of next group of d c of small motif, repeat from * 3 times, break thread.

To make napkins to match. Cut a square of linen the size desired. Over a very narrow hem work a row of s c all around and finish with the following edge.

Ch 1, skip 3 s c, 5 d c with ch 1 between each d c in next s c, ch 1, skip 3 s c, s c in next s c, repeat from beginning all around.

Make motifs following the directions of 1st 5 rows of tablecloth motif. Insert in linen cutting out the linen under the motif.

June

For the day of days make this cloth of cloths; its beauty is traditional

Materials Required—AMERICAN THREAD COMPANY "STAR" or "GEM" MERCERIZED CROCHET COTTON, Size 20

34—250 Yd. Balls White, Ecru, Cream, or Dk. Linen.

Steel Crochet Hook No. 11 or 12.

Each motif measures about 4½ inches. 204 motifs (12 x 17) are required for cloth about 54 x 72 inches.

MOTIF. Ch 8, join to form a ring, ch 6, tr c in ring, * ch 2, tr c in ring, repeat from * 13 times, ch 2, join in 4th st of ch.

2nd Row. Work 3 s c over ch 2 of each mesh, sl st in 1st s c.

3rd Row. Ch 18, s c in 2nd st from hook and work 19 s c over balance of ch, sl st in next 2 s c of center, ** ch 1, turn, work in back loop of st only for entire scroll, 1 s c in each of the next 19 s c on scroll, ch 3, turn, skip 2 sts of ch, 1 s c in next st of ch, 1 s c in each of the next 5 s c, * ch 1, turn, 1 s c in each of the next 4 s c, ch 3, turn, skip 2 sts of ch, 1 s c in next st of ch, 1 s c in each of the next 4 s c, 1 s c in each of the next 2 s c on base of scroll, repeat from * 6 times, sl st in next 4 s c of center, ch 17, turn, s c in 3rd picot from bottom of scroll just completed, ch 1, turn, and work 20 s c over ch, sl st in each of the next 2 s c of center, repeat from ** until 7 scrolls are completed. Work another scroll joining it to 1st scroll in the 6th picot, sl st in each of the next 4 s c of center, break thread.

4th Row. Attach thread to 2nd p of 5 free picots of one scroll, * ch 12, skip 1 p, s c in next p, ch 12, s c in 2nd p of next scroll, repeat from * all around, join.

5th Row. Sl st to center of loop, s c in loop, ** ch 7, sl st in 4th st from hook for p, ch 9, sl st in 4th st from hook for p, * ch 6, sl st in 4th st from hook for p, repeat from *, ch 2, skip last 3 picots, 3 tr c in 2nd ch after 1st p, holding the last loop of each tr c on needle, thread over and pull through all 4 loops on needle at one time, (a cluster st) ch 6, sl st in 4th st from hook

for p, ch 3, s c in next loop, repeat from ** all around, break thread.

Work a second motif joining in the last row as follows, sl st to center of loop, s c in loop, * ch 7, sl st in 4th st from hook for p, ch 9, sl st in 4th st from hook for p, ch 4, sl st in corresponding picot of 1st motif, ch 2, s c in 3rd ch, ch 6, sl st in 4th st from hook for p, ch 2, 3 tr c cluster st in 2nd ch after 1st p, ch 6, sl st in 4th st from hook for p, ch 3, s c in next loop, repeat from * and then finish motif same as 1st motif. Join 3rd motif to 2nd motif and 4th motif to 3rd and 1st motifs in same manner.

JOINING MOTIF. Work 1st 2 rows same as large motif.

3rd Row. * Ch 10, skip 5 s c, s c in next s c, repeat from * all around.

4th Row. Sl st in next 3 chs, s c in loop, ch 4, 2 tr c cluster st in loop, * ch 7, 3 tr c cluster st in same loop, 3 tr c cluster st in next loop, ch 7, 3 tr c cluster st in same loop, ch 7, 3 tr c cluster st in next loop, repeat from * twice, ch 7, 3 tr c cluster st in same loop, 3 tr c cluster st in next loop, ch 7, 3 tr c cluster st in same loop, ch 7, join in top of cluster st.

5th Row. Ch 2, sl st in center free picot of motif, ch 2, sl st in top of cluster st, 7 s c in loop, 1 s c between cluster sts, 7 s c in next loop, 1 s c in cluster st, ch 2, sl st in next center picot of same motif, ch 2, sl st in s c, s c in next loop, ch 7, sl st in 4th st from hook for p, ch 9, sl st in 4th st from hook for p, ch 3, sl st between joinings, ch 2, sl st in 2nd ch, ch 6, sl st in 4th st from hook for p, ch 2, 3 tr c cluster st in 2nd ch after 1st p, ch 6, sl st in 4th st from hook for p, ch 3, s c in same loop, s c in cluster st, repeat from beginning until all joinings are completed, break thread.

Suggestions for napkins to match. Cut squares of linen any size desired allowing ¾ inch for hemstitching. Draw 6 or more threads ¾ inch from edge. Baste hem meeting the drawn threads. Working on the wrong side and beginning at left of hem, pick up 4 or 5 threads (from right to left) pull needle through, tighten and make a second st in the hem, pick up the next 4 or 5 threads, pull thread through and fasten with a second st. Repeat all around.

Crocheted Motif. Repeat 1st and 2nd rows of motif then repeat 3rd row working 4 scrolls only. Over remainder of ring work a row of s c working a picot after every 3rd st. Applique to one corner of napkin.

July

Simple decorations. Simple place settings. Make it in Red and White to pep up drooping Summer spirits

Materials Required—AMERICAN THREAD COMPANY "SILLATEEN SANSIL"

8—210 Yd. Balls Red or any contrasting color desired.
5—210 Yd. Balls Cream or White.
Steel Crochet Hook No. 10.
Each plate mat measures 10½ x 17½.

GAUGE: 5 shells sts = 2 inches.   11 rows = 2 inches.

With Color, ch 4, 3 d c in 4th st from hook, ch 3, turn, 2 d c in 1st d c, skip 1 d c, sl st in next d c, ch 3, 2 d c in same space with sl st, ch 3, turn.

3rd Row. 2 d c in 1st d c, sl st in ch 3 of same shell in previous row, ch 3, 2 d c in same space, sl st in ch 3 of next shell, ch 3, 2 d c in same space, ch 3, turn. Repeat 3rd row having one more shell in each row and ending each row with 2 d c in same space until there are 18 shells in row. The straight sides should now measure about 4 inches, break thread.

Attach Cream and continue in same manner until there are 39 shells in row. The straight sides should now measure about 9 inches, break thread.

Attach Color and continue in same manner until there are 49 shells in row. Straight side should now measure about 11 inches.

Next row. End with a sl st in last shell, ch 1, turn.

Next Row. Sl st to ch 3 of shell, ch 3, work a shell in same space and continue shells to end of row. There should be 49 shells in each row. Repeat these 2 rows working 7 more rows in Color, break thread. Attach Cream and continue in same manner until long side measures about 15½ inches, ending on short side, break thread.

Attach Color and continue in same manner for 10 rows.

Next Row. Sl st to ch 3 at beginning of row and end row in ch 3 of last shell. Repeat last row working 8 more rows in Color, break thread.

Attach Cream and continue in same manner until there are 19 shells in row, break thread.

Attach Color and continue in same manner until 2 shells remain, ch 1, turn, sl st to ch of shell, ch 3, thread over, insert in same space and work off 2 loops. * thread over, insert in next d c of shell and work off 2 loops, repeat from *, thread over and work off all loops at one time, ch 1, break thread and fasten securely.

Work a row of shells all around working Cream into Cream and Color into Color.

15

August

Filet Crochet for icy crispness. Use pastel colors for the center. Note how effectively a garden vegetable can enhance the gayety of your table

Materials Required—AMERICAN THREAD COMPANY "STAR" or "GEM" MERCERIZED CROCHET COTTON, Size 20, White

11—250 Yd. Balls.

Steel Crochet Hook No. 12 or 13.

¼ Yd. Linen.

Each plate mat measures 15½ x 18.

Starting at arrow marked A, ch 84 and work 1 d c in 9th st from hook, ch 2, skip 2 chs, 1 d c in each of the next 67 chs, ch 2, skip 2 chs, d c in next ch, ch 2, skip 2 chs, d c in next ch, ch 5, turn.

2nd Row. D c in next d c, ch 2, 1 d c in each of the next 4 d c, * ch 2, skip 2 d c, d c in next d c, repeat from * 19 times, 1 d c in each of the next 3 dc, ch 2, d c in next d c, ch 2, d c in 3rd st of ch, ch 5, turn.

3rd Row. D c in next d c, ch 2, 1 d c in each of the next 4 d c, ch 2 and work 21 open meshes, 2 d c in next mesh, d c in d c, ch 2, d c in 3rd st of ch, ch 2, d tr c in same space, (this is an increase) ch 5, turn and work up and down according to diagram working to arrow B, continue corner and break thread.

Attach thread at arrow C and work 25 open meshes, ch 5, turn and work back and forth according to diagram between arrow C and D. Repeat between C and D once then work another corner.

Repeat between arrow C and D 3 times and work a corner. Repeat between arrow C and D twice, work a corner. Repeat between arrow C and D twice joining the work together in the last 2 rows by working 1st into the last row then into the 1st row until entire side is joined.

EDGE. Work a row of s c all around working 2 s c in each 2 ch mesh and 2 s c, ch 3, 2 s c in each 5 ch mesh. Fit a piece of material into the opening allowing for a narrow hem. Sew to filet edge on right side keeping center flat. Turn a narrow hem and sew again on the wrong side.

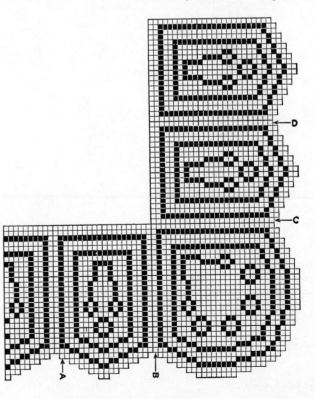

September

Happy Birthday to you — and you — and you if you own this cloth. Use real roses for decoration

Materials Required—AMERICAN THREAD COMPANY "STAR" or "GEM" MERCERIZED CROCHET COTTON, Size 30

29--325 Yd. Balls, White, Cream, Ercu or Dark Linen.

Each motif measures about 4 inches. 234 motifs 13x18 are required for cloth measuring 52 x 72 inches.

Steel Crochet Hook No. 12 or 13.

MOTIF. Ch 6, s c in 5th st from hook for a picot, * ch 7, s c in 5th st from hook for a picot, repeat from * 6 times, ch 1, drop loop off hook, insert in 1st ch made and pull loop through forming a circle and having all picots on inside of circle.

2nd Row. Ch 3, 2 d c in same space, 1 d c in base of picot, * 5 d c over next 2 ch loop between picots, d c in base of next picot, repeat from * 6 times, 2 d c in first loop, join in 3rd st of ch.

3rd Row. Ch 19, 1 d c in 5th st from hook, 1 d c in each of the next 10 chs, 1 d c in next st, 1 s d c in same st, (s d c, thread over hook, insert in st and work off all loops at one time) skip 1 d c of previous row, d c in next d c, * ch 11, turn, join to top of petal just made by working 1 d c in the 4th st of ch at top of petal, ch 4, turn, 1 d c in d c just made, 1 d c in each of the next 10 chs, d c in next st, s d c in same space, skip 1 d c of previous row, d c in next st, repeat from * all around, join to 1st ch 3, break thread. (24 petals.)

4th Row. Join thread to corner of last petal, ch 3, sl st in corner of 1st petal completing circle. Sl st into 4 ch loop at top of petal, ch 6, 1 d c in same space, * ch 2, 1 s c in space between petals, ch 2, 1 d c in top of next petal, ch 3, 1 d c in same space, repeat from * all around ending with ch 2, s c in next loop, ch 2, join.

5th Row. Sl st into center st of 3 ch loop, s c in same st, ** ch 8, sl st in 5th st from hook for picot, ch 3, s c in same st with last s c, ch 4, 1 tr c in center of next shell, * ch 5, sl st in 4th st from hook for picot, ch 1, tr c in same loop, repeat from * twice, ch 4, s c in center st of next shell, repeat from ** all around, join, break thread.

6th Row. Join thread to center picot of shell, ** ch 4, skip 1 picot of shell, d c in picot of long ch loop, * ch 5, sl st in 4th st from hook for picot, ch 1, d c in same space, repeat from * 5 times, ch 4, s c in center picot of next shell, repeat from ** all around, join, break thread.

Work a second motif in same manner joining it to 1st motif in last row as follows; join thread in center picot of shell, ch 4, d c in picot between shells, ch 1, picot, ch 1, d c in same space, ch 1, picot, ch 1, d c in same space, * ch 3, join to corresponding picot of 1st motif, ch 2, sl st in 2nd st of ch, ch 1, d c in same space of 2nd motif, repeat from *, ch 1, picot, ch 1, d c in same space, ch 1, picot, ch 1, d c in same space, ch 4, s c in center picot of next shell, ch 4, d c in picot between shells, and

join another shell in same manner, finish row same as 1st motif.

Join 3rd motif to 2nd motif leaving 1 shell free to fill in later. Join 4th motif to 3rd and 1st motifs in same manner.

JOINING MOTIF. Ch 10, join to form a ring, ch 1 and work 16 s c into ring.

2nd Row. Ch 5, d c in next s c, * ch 2, d c in next s c, repeat from * all around, ch 2, join in 3rd st of ch 5.

3rd Row. Ch 1 and work 3 s c in each space.

4th Row. * Ch 8, skip 6 s c, s c over the d c of 2nd row, repeat from * all around.

5th Row. Ch 1, * 3 s c in next loop, ch 4, 2 s c in same loop, ch 4, 3 s c in same loop, 2 s c, 4 d c, ch 4, 4 d c, 2 s c in next loop, repeat from * all around, join.

6th Row. Ch 4, s c in 4 ch picot loop, ch 2, join to 3rd picot of shell of large motif, ch 2, complete picot, ch 3, s c in next 4 ch picot loop of small motif, ch 2, join to 4th picot of same shell of large motif, ch 2, complete picot, ch 4, s c in s c between scallops of small motif, ch 4, tr c in 4 ch picot loop at corner of small motif, ch 1, picot, ch 1, tr c in same loop, ch 1, picot, ch 1, d tr c in same loop, ch 4, sl st in joining of large motifs, ch 4, s c in top of d tr c just made, ch 1, picot, ch 1, tr c in same space of small motif, ch 1, picot, ch 1, tr c in same space, ch 4, s c in s c between scallops of small motif, repeat from beginning all around.

To make linen napkins to match. Cut squares of linen the desired size and over a very narrow hem work a row of s c with a ch 4 picot after every 5th s c.

MOTIF. Work the first 5 rows of joining motif.

6th Row. * Ch 4, s c in next ch 4 picot loop, ch 6, sl st in 4th st from hook for picot, ch 2, s c in next 4 ch picot loop, ch 4, s c in s c between scallops, ch 4, d c in next ch 4 picot loop of next scallop, ch 4, sl st in top of d c just made, ch 2, tr c in same space, ch 4, sl st in top of tr c just made, ch 2, d tr c in same space, picot, ch 2, tr c in same space, picot, ch 2, d c in same space, picot, ch 4, s c in s c between scallops, repeat from * all around, break thread and applique to corner of napkin.

19

October

Autumn stripes for Halloween. Very simple filet crochet in fascinating colors

**Materials Required—AMERICAN THREAD COMPANY
"GEM" MERCERIZED CROCHET COTTON
Size 30**

9—400 Yd. Balls Cream.
4—300 Yd. Balls Yellow.
5—300 Yd. Balls Green.
Steel Crochet Hook No. 11 or 12.
This will make a cloth 45 x 60.

With **Cream,** crochet a ch about 70 inches long, d c in 8th st from hook, * ch 2, skip 2 chs, d c in next ch, repeat from * across row until cloth measures 60 inches, having a multiple of 6 meshes for each pattern plus 3 meshes at end of row. If a longer cloth is desired crochet a longer ch.

2nd Row. Ch 5, turn, d c in next d c, * ch 2, d c in next d c, repeat from * 3 times, 2 d c in mesh, d c in next d c, * work 5 open meshes, 1 solid mesh, repeat from * across row ending with 3 open meshes, ch 5, turn.

3rd Row. 4 open meshes, 1 solid mesh, * 5 open meshes, 1 solid mesh, repeat from * across row ending row with 4 open meshes, ch 5, turn.

4th Row. 3 open meshes, * 1 solid mesh, 5 open meshes, repeat from * across row having 5 open meshes at end of row, ch 5, turn and work 3 rows of open meshes. Repeat from 2nd row until there are 46 rows, break thread. Attach Green and work 3 rows of open meshes, continue in pattern same as Cream until there are 15 rows of Green, break thread.

Attach Yellow and work 15 rows in pattern, break thread.

Attach Green and work 15 rows in pattern, break thread.

Attach Cream and repeat from 2nd row twice.

Attach Cream and work 46 rows in pattern, break thread.

SCALLOP. With Cream and working across short side, attach thread in mesh before corner mesh, ch 4, tr c in same space, ch 3, thread over needle twice, insert in same space and work off 2 loops twice, thread over needle twice, insert in same space and work off 2 loops twice, thread over needle and work off remaining loops at one time (cluster st) ch 3, cluster st in same space, ch 3, cluster st in corner mesh, ch 7, cluster st in same mesh, ch 3, 3 cluster sts with ch 3 between each cluster st in next mesh, * ch 3, skip 1 mesh, sl st in next mesh, ch 3, skip 1 mesh, 3 cluster sts with ch 3 between each cluster st in next mesh, repeat from * all around working all corners to correspond.

Napkins to match may be made of colored linen, Green and Yellow. Cut squares of linen in both colors any size desired and roll a narrow hem. Work a row of s c all around, then work 1 row of open meshes and finish with scallop same as cloth.

November

The Grape Leaf Pattern is especially appropriate for this time of year. We would like it for "January-February-June or July" too

Materials Required—AMERICAN THREAD COMPANY "STAR" or "GEM" MERCERIZED CROCHET COTTON, Size 20

44—250 Yd. Balls White or Colors.

3 Skeins "Star" Six Strand Mercerized Embroidery Cotton, White, for initial on napkins.

Steel Crochet Hook No. 11 or 12.

This will make a cloth 56 x 72.

Each Motif measures about 4½ inches.

CHART No. 1. Ch. 80, work 1st d c in 8th st from hook, 1 d c in each of the next 3 sts, ch 2, skip 2 sts, 1 d c in each of the next 4 sts, * ch 2, skip 2 sts, d c in next st, ch 2, skip 2 sts, 1 d c in each of the next 10 sts, repeat from * twice, ch 2, skip 2 sts, d c in next st, ch 2, skip 2 sts, 1 d c in each of the next 4 sts, ch 2, skip 2 sts, 1 d c in each of the next 4 sts, ch 2 skip 2 sts, d c in next st, ch 3, turn and work back and forth according to diagram. Work a row of s c all around motif and work 129 more motifs.

CHART No. 2. Ch 80, work 1st d c in 8th ch from hook and continue back and forth according to diagram No. 2, finish with a row of s c all around and work 19 more motifs for the ends of cloth. For the sides of cloth work 26 motifs working up and down on diagram No. 2.

Follow Chart No. 3 for the corners, work two squares up and down according to diagram and 2 squares back and forth according to diagram. Sew all squares together as illustrated matching the rows.

EDGE. Join thread in corner, 1 s c in each of the next 12 s c, ch 5, turn, s c in 6th s c from hook, ch 5, s c in 1st s c made, ch 1, turn and work 9 s c over first ch 5 loop and 5 s c over second loop, ch 5, turn, s c in center st of 1st scallop, ch 1, turn and work 5 s c over loop, picot, 4 s c over same loop, sl st in top of 2nd scallop and finish that scallop with 4 more s c, sl st into s c of previous row and repeat from beginning all around.

If napkins to match are desired cut squares of linen the size required and over a rolled hem work a row of s c. Finish with edge same as on cloth.

Transfer initial in corner and embroider in Satin Stitch.

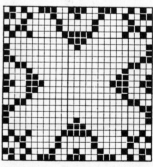

1

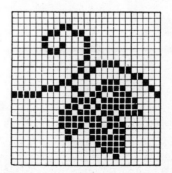

2

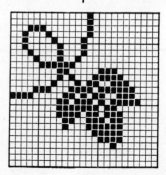

3

December

Smart — is the one word to describe this insertion. A wonderful background for any meal

Materials Required—AMERICAN THREAD COMPANY "STAR" or "GEM" MERCERIZED CROCHET

COTTON, Size 20

11—250 Yd. Balls will make 2 stripes 90 inches long and the edging around Cloth.

Steel Crochet Hook No. 12 or 13.

3 Skeins of "Star" Six Strand Mercerized Embroidery Cotton, White for initials on napkins.

2½ Yds. of 45 inch Linen will make a cloth 64½ x 92½.

INSERTION. Ch 101, d c in 8th st from hook, * ch 2, skip 2 sts, d c in next st, repeat from * to end of ch (32 meshes) ch 5, turn.

2nd Row. D c in next d c, * ch 5, s c in next d c, ch 5, d c in next d c, repeat from * 5 times, * ch 2, d c in next d c, repeat from * 5 times, * ch 5, s c in next d c, ch 5, d c in next d c, repeat from * 5 times, ch 2, d c in 3rd st of ch at end of row, ch 5, turn.

3rd Row. D c in d c, * ch 5, d c in next d c, repeat from * 5 times, ch 2, d c in next d c, * 2 d c in mesh, d c in d c, repeat from * 3 times, ch 2, d c in next d c, * ch 5, d c in next d c, repeat from * 5 times, ch 2,

d c in 3rd st of ch 5 at end of row, ch 5, turn. Continue working up and down according to diagram until insertion measures about 90 inches or length desired. Complete a pattern and end with a row of open meshes. Work a second length of insertion and finish edges with a row of s c. Insert lace into linen sewing it on the right side first then turn a very narrow hem and sew on the wrong side.

EDGING. Work a row of s c over a rolled hem around the linen sections, then work a row of 2 ch meshes all around working 2 d c with ch 3 between in each corner.

2nd Row. Work 5 s c in each corner mesh and 2 s c in each mesh on sides of cloth then work a row of meshes.

4th Row. 3 s c in each of the next 2 meshes, * ch 4, sl st in top of last s c for picot, 3 s c in each of the next 2 meshes and repeat from * all around.

To Make Napkins to Match. Cut linen the size desired. Work a row of s c over a rolled hem and work border same as on cloth. Stamp initial in corner and embroider in satin stitch with "Star" Six Strand.

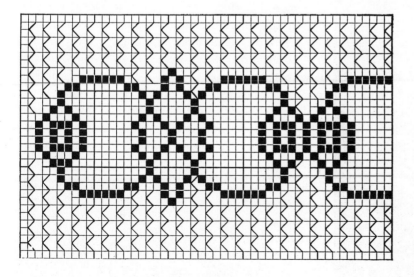

Banquet Beauty

MATERIALS:

J. & P. COATS or CLARK'S O.N.T. BEST SIX CORD MERCERIZED CROCHET, *Size 30:*

SMALL BALL:

J. & P. COATS —26 balls of White or Ecru,
OR   or 35 balls of any color.

CLARK'S O.N.T.—42 balls of White, Ecru
or any color.

BIG BALL:

J. & P. COATS —13 balls of White or Ecru.

Steel Crochet Hook No. 10 or 11.

Tablecloth about 80 x 100 inches

GAUGE: 5 sps make 1 inch; 5 rows make 1 inch.

Starting at bottom of chart, make a chain 2½ yards long (14 ch sts to 1 inch). **1st row:** Dc in 8th ch from hook (sp made), ch 2, skip 2 ch, dc in next ch (another sp made). Make 6 more sps, then work * dc in each of next 33 ch (11 bls made), work 13 sps. Repeat from * 14 more times; work dc in next 33 ch, then work 8 sps. Cut off remaining chain. Ch 5, turn. **2nd row:** Dc in next dc, ch 2, dc in next dc (sp made over sp). Make 3 more sps, 2 dc in next sp, dc in next dc (bl made over sp), make 2 more bls, then work dc in next 3 dc (bl made over bl). Work dc in each dc of dc group, then work bl over each of the next 3 sps (18 bls in all). * Work 7 sps, 18 bls. Repeat from * across, ending with 18 bls, 4 sps, then ch 2, skip 2 ch of turning ch, dc in next ch. Ch 5, turn. **3rd row:** Work 4 sps, 4 bls, ch 2, skip 2 dc, dc in next dc (sp made over bl). Work 10 more sps, * 4 bls, 5 sps, 4 bls, 12 sps. Repeat from * across, ending with 11 sps, 4 bls, 4 sps.

Starting with 4th row, follow chart to top. Chart shows one quarter of design. To make second half of each row, do not repeat center sp or bl, as the case may be, but work back. When top row is reached, do not repeat top row, but reverse the design by working back to the 1st row. Fasten off.

Block to measurements given.

There are 10 spaces between heavy lines   Start here

CANDLEGLOW

62 x 81 inches

Candleglow

MATERIALS:

CLARK'S BIG BALL MERCERIZED CROCHET, *Size 30:*

20 balls of White or Ecru; or 25 balls of any color.

Steel Crochet Hook No. 10 or 11.

GAUGE: Each motif measures about 3¼ inches in diameter.

For a tablecloth about 62 x 81 inches, make 19 x 25 motifs.

FIRST MOTIF . . . Ch 9, join with sl st to form ring. **1st rnd:** Ch 1, 24 sc in ring. Join with sl st in 1st sc made. **2nd rnd:** Ch 4 (to count as 1 tr), holding back the last loop of each tr on hook make tr in each of next 2 sc, thread over and draw through all loops on hook (3-tr cluster made), * ch 7, make a 3-tr cluster over the next 3 sc. Repeat from * around, joining last ch-7 with sl st in top of 1st cluster. **3rd rnd:** Sl st in 3 ch, ch 1, sc in same loop, * ch 8, sc in next loop. Repeat from * around, joining last ch-8 with sl st in 1st sc. **4th rnd:** Sl st in loop, ch 4, in same loop make three 4-tr clusters with ch 5 between, * ch 5, in next loop make three 4-tr clusters with ch 5 between. Repeat from * around. Join. **5th rnd:** Sl st in 2 ch, ch 1, sc in same loop, * ch 5, sc in next loop. Repeat from * around. Join. **6th rnd:** Ch 1, * 7 sc in next loop, 3 sc in next loop, ch 7, turn, sl st in center sc of last loop, turn; in ch-7 loop make 5 sc, ch 5 and 5 sc, 3 sc in re- mainder of loop. Repeat from * around. Join and fasten off.

SECOND MOTIF . . . Work as for 1st motif until 5th rnd is complete. **6th rnd:** Ch 1, * 7 sc in next loop, 3 sc in next loop, ch 7, turn, sl st in center sc of last loop, turn; 5 sc in ch-7 loop, ch 2, sc in cor- responding ch-5 loop on 1st motif, ch 2, 5 sc in same loop on 2nd motif, 3 sc in remainder of loop. Repeat from * once more. Complete rnd as for 1st motif (no more joinings).

Make necessary number of motifs and join 2 loops of each motif to 2 loops of adjacent motifs, leaving 1 loop free on each motif between joinings.

FILL-IN MOTIF . . . Ch 9 and work 1st and 2nd rnds of 1st motif. **3rd rnd:** Ch 1, * 3 sc in next loop, ch 9, sc in joining of motifs, ch 9, 3 sc in same loop on Fill-in motif, 3 sc in next loop, ch 2, sc in next free ch-5 loop on motif, ch 2, 3 sc in same loop on Fill-in motif. Repeat from * around. Join and fasten off.

Work fill-in motifs in this manner in all sps be- tween joinings.

KITCHEN CHECKS

36 inches square

Come-Into-the-Kitchen

MATERIALS:

J. & P. COATS KNIT-CRO-SHEEN,

4 balls of White and 7 balls of Color.

Steel Crochet Hook No. 6.

Cloth measures 36 x 36 inches, excluding fringe.

GAUGE: 10 sts make 1 inch; 8 rows make 1 inch.

Starting at one edge with Color, make a 39-inch chain (about 10 ch sts to 1 inch). **1st row:** In order to conceal it, hold White on top of chain, work sc over it in 2nd ch from hook and in next 6 ch; * insert hook in next ch and pull loop through, drop Color, pick up White and draw through both loops on hook, thus changing color. Holding Color on top of chain, work sc over it in each of the next 7 ch, insert hook in next ch and pull loop through, drop White, pick up Color and draw through both loops on hook. Holding White on top of chain, work sc over it in each of next 7 ch. Repeat from * across until there are 23 Color groups and 22 White groups. Fasten off, leaving 4-inch lengths of both colors. These lengths will be used later for Fringe. **2nd row:** Leaving 4-inch lengths of both colors free, attach threads in 1st sc of last row. Working over unused color in order to conceal it and changing color as before, ch 1 and make Color sc in back loop of each Color sc and White sc in back loop of each White sc across. Fasten off, leaving 4-inch lengths of both colors. Repeat 2nd row 4 more times. This completes 1st row of blocks. **Next row:** Work as before only make White sc's over Color sc's and Color sc's over White sc's. Work 5 more rows in pattern as established by last row. This com-

pletes 2nd row of blocks. Continue thus, alternating 1st and 2nd rows of blocks until piece is square, ending with 1st row of blocks. Fasten off.

FRINGE . . . There are two 4-inch lengths (1 White and 1 Color) at both ends of each row. Insert hook at base of an sc on one edge and pull a loop (both lengths) through. Draw free ends through this loop and pull tight. Work each set of 4-inch lengths in this manner. To make Fringe on the 2 remaining edges, cut one 8-inch length of Color. Fold this length in half, insert hook from right side in corner st and pull Color loop through; draw one free end through loop and pull tight. * Take an 8-inch length of White and fold in half, insert hook in next st and pull a loop consisting of the remaining end of previous Color length and this White length through, then draw the Color strand and 1 strand of White through this loop. Take an 8-inch length of Color and fold in half, insert hook in next st and pull loop consisting of the remaining end of previous White length and this Color length through, then draw the White strand and 1 strand of Color through this loop. Repeat from * across. Then work Fringe on remaining edge. Trim all Fringe to measure 2 inches. Press through damp cloth.

31

MOUNTAIN LAUREL

63 x 82 inches

Motif shows edging used around completed cloth.

Mountain Laurel

MATERIALS:

CLARK'S BIG BALL MERCERIZED CROCHET, *Size 20:*
24 balls of White or Ecru.
Steel Crochet Hook No. 9 or 10.

GAUGE: Each motif measures 4½ inches in diameter.

For a tablecloth about 63 x 82 inches, make 364 motifs.

FIRST MOTIF . . . Starting at center, ch 8. Join with sl st to form ring. **1st rnd:** Ch 3 (to count as 1 dc), 23 dc in ring. Join with sl st in top st of ch-3. **2nd rnd:** Ch 3, dc in each of next 3 dc, * ch 4, dc in each of next 4 dc. Repeat from * around, joining last ch-4 with sl st in top st of ch-3. **3rd rnd:** Ch 3, dc in same place as sl st, * dc in next 2 dc, 2 dc in next dc, ch 5, 2 dc in next dc. Repeat from * around. Join. **4th rnd:** Ch 3, dc in same place as sl st, * dc in next 2 dc, ch 3, dc in next 2 dc, 2 dc in next dc, ch 6, 2 dc in next dc. Repeat from * around. Join. **5th rnd:** Ch 3, dc in same place as sl st, * dc in next 2 dc, ch 5, skip 2 dc, dc in next 2 dc, 2 dc in next dc, ch 7, 2 dc in next dc. Repeat from * around. Join. **6th rnd:** Ch 3, skip next dc, dc in next 2 dc, * ch 3, dc in next 3 dc, ch 5, 4 dc in next loop, ch 5, skip next dc, dc in next 3 dc. Repeat from * around. Join. **7th rnd:** Ch 3, skip next dc, dc in next dc, * 2 dc in next sp, dc in next 2 dc, ch 6, skip next dc, 2 dc in next dc, dc in next 2 dc, 2 dc in next dc, ch 6, skip next dc, dc in next 2 dc. Repeat from * around. Join. **8th rnd:** Ch 3, skip next dc, dc in next 3 dc, * ch 7, skip next dc, 2 dc in next dc, dc in next 2 dc, ch 3, dc in next 2 dc, 2 dc in next dc, ch 7, skip next dc, dc in next 4 dc. Repeat from * around. Join. **9th rnd:** Sl st in next 2 dc, ch 11, * skip next dc, 2 dc in next dc, dc in next 3 dc, ch 4, dc in next 3 dc, 2 dc in next dc, ch 8, skip 2 dc, dc in next dc, ch 8. Repeat from * around. Join last ch-8 with sl st in 3rd st of ch-11. **10th rnd:** Ch 8, dc in same place as sl st, * ch 9, 2 dc in next dc, dc in next 4 dc, ch 5, dc in next 4 dc, 2 dc in next dc, ch 9, in next dc make dc,

ch 5 and dc. Repeat from * around. Join and fasten off.

SECOND MOTIF . . . Work as for 1st motif until 9th rnd is completed. **10th rnd:** Ch 8, dc in same place as sl st, ch 5, sc in 5th st of corresponding ch-9 on 1st motif, ch 3, 2 dc in next dc on 2nd motif, dc in next 4 dc, ch 2, sc in center ch of next ch-5 on 1st motif, ch 2, dc in next 4 dc on 2nd motif, 2 dc in next dc, ch 3, sc in 3rd st of corresponding ch-9 on 1st motif, ch 5, in next dc on 2nd motif make dc, ch 5 and dc and complete rnd as for 1st motif (no more joinings).

Make 364 motifs in all and join them as in diagram for joining hexagon motifs on page 50, having 27 motifs from A to B and 13 motifs from A to C.

EDGING . . . With right side facing attach thread in first ch-5 sp (from joining) on end motif of narrow edge. **1st rnd:** Ch 6 (to count as tr and ch 2), in same sp make 5 tr with ch 2 between (6-tr shell made), * (sc in next loop, tr in next 6 dc, ch 2, make a 6-tr shell in next sp, ch 2, tr in next 6 dc, sc in next loop, make a 6-tr shell in next sp) 3 times, making last sc in joining of motifs, shell in next sp. Repeat from * across narrow end, then continue in this manner all around cloth. Join with sl st in 4th st of starting chain. **2nd rnd:** Sl st across to 2nd ch-2 sp, ch 1, sc in same sp, ** (ch 5, sc in next sp) 3 times; * ch 5, skip 2 dc, sc in next dc, (ch 5, sc in next sp) 7 times; ch 5, skip 3 dc, sc in next dc, (ch 5, sc in next sp) 5 times. Repeat from * once more, ch 5, skip 2 dc, sc in next dc (ch 5, sc in next sp) 7 times; ch 5, skip 3 dc, sc in next dc, (ch 5, sc in next sp) 4 times; sc in 2nd sp on next shell. Repeat from ** across narrow end, then continue in this manner all around cloth. Join and fasten off.

Peasant Pottery

MATERIALS:

J. & P. COATS CROCHET CORD,

11 balls of main color (White or Ecru),

2 balls of 1st color and 3 balls of 2nd color.

Steel Crochet Hook No. 1.

This amount of material is sufficient for a set of 4 place mats, each 12 x 16½ inches, and a runner, 12 x 33 inches, including fringe.

GAUGE: 3 shells make 3 inches; 5 rows of shells make 2 inches.

PLACE MAT (Make 4) . . . Starting at long edge with main color, make a chain about 25 inches long. **1st row:** Sc in 2nd ch from hook, * skip 4 ch, 7 tr in next ch (shell made), skip 4 ch, sc in next ch. Repeat from * across, until 13 shells have been made, ending with an sc (row should measure about 13½ inches). Cut off remaining chain. Ch 4, turn. **2nd row:** 3 tr in 1st sc (half shell made), * sc in center tr of next shell, shell in next sc. Repeat from * across, ending with 4 tr in last sc (half shell made). Ch 1, turn. **3rd row:** Sc in 1st tr, * shell in next sc, sc in center tr of next shell. Repeat from * across, ending with sc in top st of turning ch. Fasten off. Attach 1st color, ch 4, turn. **4th row:** Same as 2nd row. Fasten off. Attach 2nd color, ch 1, turn. **5th row:** Same as 3rd row. Fasten off. Attach main color, ch 4, turn. **6th row:** Same as 2nd row. Ch 1, turn. **7th row:** Same as 3rd row but do not fasten off. Ch 4, turn. **8th row:** Same as 2nd row. **9th and 10th rows:** Repeat 7th and 2nd rows. **11th row:** Sc in 1st tr, (shell in next sc, sc in center tr of next shell) twice. Change color by drawing a loop of 1st color through loop on hook. Fasten off main color. Shell in next sc. Change to main color as before and fasten off 1st color. Work sc in center tr of next shell and continue in pattern across until 3 shells of main color have been completed, change to 2nd color as before and work a shell. Change to main color and make 3 shells;

then make a shell of 1st color and complete row with main color. Ch 4, turn. **12th row:** Half shell in 1st sc, sc in center tr of next shell, shell in next sc, sc in center tr of next shell. Change to 1st color. Fasten off main color and work 2 shells; change to main color and work 2 shells; change to 2nd color and work 2 shells; change to main color and work 2 shells; change to 1st color and work 2 shells; complete row with main color. Ch 1, turn. **13th row:** (This is center row of Mat.) Sc in 1st tr, shell in next sc, sc in center tr of next shell; now make 3 shells with 1st color, 1 shell with main color, 3 shells with 2nd color, 1 shell with main color, 3 shells with 1st color and 1 shell with main color. Ch 4, turn. **14th and 15th rows:** Same as 12th and 11th rows. Now work 5 rows of shells with main color, 1 row with 2nd color, 1 row with 1st color and 3 rows with main color. Fasten off.

FRINGE . . . Cut two 4-inch strands of main color. Double these strands forming a loop. Insert hook in a stitch at edge of Mat and pull loop through; now draw loose ends through loop and pull tightly. Make fringe closely all around. Trim fringe to measure 1½ inches.

RUNNER . . . With main color make a chain about 40 inches long and work as for 1st row of Place Mat until there are 29 shells on the row. Cut off remaining chain. Ch 4, turn. Now work as for Place Mat, making 7 diamonds (instead of 3) across center of Runner, alternating colors as before. Make fringe all around Runner same as on Place Mat.

Centerpiece 22½ inches square.

W itching hour . . . sparkling crystal, gleaming silver, fine damask . . . and queenly filet! Where could you find a more gracious foursome to mix serene dignity with warm hospitality for your formal affairs? . . . a handsome gift for a special friend too!

Filet Centerpiece

MATERIALS:

J. & P. COATS or CLARK'S O.N.T. BEST SIX CORD MERCERIZED CROCHET, *Size 50:*

J. & P. COATS—8 balls of White or Ecru   OR   CLARK'S O.N.T.—13 balls of White or Ecru.

Steel Crochet Hook No. 12.

GAUGE: 6 sps make 1 inch; 6 rows make 1 inch.

Starting at bottom of chart make a chain 25 inches long (17 ch sts to 1 inch). **1st row:** Dc in 8th ch from hook, * ch 2, skip 2 ch, dc in next ch. Repeat from * across until there are 131 sps made. Cut off remaining chain. Ch 5, turn. **2nd row:** Dc in next dc, (2 dc in next sp, dc in next dc) 8 times (8 bls over 8 sps made); (ch 2, dc in next dc) 9 times (9 sps over 9 sps made); make 3 bls, 3 sps, 2 bls, 13 sps, 1 bl, 25 sps, 1 bl, 25 sps, 1 bl, 13 sps, 2 bls, 3 sps, 3 bls, 9 sps, 8 bls, ch 2, skip 2 sts of turning ch, dc in next ch. Ch 5, turn. **3rd row:** Dc in next dc, dc in next 3 dc (bl over bl made); (ch 2,

skip 2 dc, dc in next dc) 7 times (7 sps over 7 bls made); make 3 bls, 5 sps, 5 bls, 1 sp, 4 bls, 11 sps, 2 bls, (2 sps, 3 bls) twice; 4 sps, 2 bls, 8 sps, 3 bls, 8 sps, 2 bls, 4 sps, (3 bls, 2 sps) twice; 2 bls, 11 sps, 4 bls, 1 sp, 5 bls, 5 sps, 3 bls, 7 sps, 1 bl, 1 sp. Ch 5, turn. **Note:** Chart shows one quarter of design. Starting with 4th row follow chart. To complete each row omit center sp or bl, as the case may be, and work back from center to beginning of row. When top of chart is reached, reverse chart, omit last (center) row and work back to 1st row. Do not fasten off but turn and work edging all around as follows: **1st rnd:** Ch 16 (to count as dc and ch 13), holding back the last loop of each dc on hook make dc in top of last dc made, dc in next dc, thread over and draw through all loops on hook (2-dc cluster made), * * ch 10, 2-dc cluster over next 2 dc, * ch 10, skip next dc, 2-dc cluster over next 2 dc. Repeat from * across to last 2 sps, ch 10, dc in next dc and in center st of corner sp, working off the 2 dc as before, ch 13, dc in same place as last dc, dc in next dc, working off the 2 dc as before (this is corner loop). Repeat from * * around, ending with dc in last dc, sl st in 3rd st of starting chain. **2nd rnd:** In each corner loop make 5 sc, (ch 3, 3 sc) twice, ch 3 and 5 sc; in all other loops make (3 sc, ch 3) 3 times and 3 sc, ending with sl st in 1st sc made. Fasten off.

Starch lightly and block to measurement given.

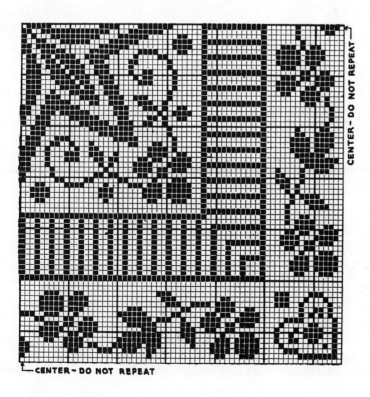

There are 10 spaces between heavy lines.

There's a wondrous sweep of magnificence woven into this maze of crisp medallions . . . made to spread like a glorious constellation from the head of your table to the foot!

Tablecloth 54 x 74 inches.

MATERIALS:

J. & P. COATS or CLARK'S O.N.T. BEST SIX CORD MERCERIZED CROCHET, *Size 30:*

SMALL BALL:

J. & P. COATS —48 balls of White or Ecru,
OR   or 63 balls of any color.
CLARK'S O.N.T.—76 balls of White, Ecru
     or any color.

BIG BALL:

J. & P. COATS —24 balls of White or Ecru.

Steel Crochet Hook No. 10 or 11.

GAUGE: Motif measures about 3⅜ inches in diameter after blocking.

FIRST MOTIF . . . Ch 7. Join with sl st to form ring. **1st rnd:** Ch 3 to count as 1 dc, 23 dc in ring. Join with sl st in top st of 1st ch-3. **2nd rnd:** (Ch 5, skip next dc, sc in next dc) 11 times; ch 2, skip next dc, dc in next dc. **3rd and 4th rnds:** (Ch 5, sc in next loop) 11 times; ch 2, dc in next loop. **5th rnd:** Ch 1, work 7 sc in each loop around. Join with sl st in 1st sc. **6th rnd:** Sl st across to 4th sc of scallop, * ch 8, 5 dc in 3rd ch from hook, ch 2, sl st in same ch where dc's were made, ch 5, sc in 4th sc of next scallop. Repeat from * around, joining last ch-5 at base of 1st ch. Fasten off. **7th rnd:** Attach thread in center st of any dc group of last rnd, * ch 11, sc in center st of next dc group. Repeat from * around. Join. **8th rnd:** Ch 1, work 15 sc in each loop around. Join. **9th rnd:** Skip 1st sc, * sc in next 6 sc, in next sc make sc, ch 3 and sc; sc in next 6 sc, skip 2 sc. Repeat from * around. Join. **10th rnd:** Skip 1st sc, * sc in next 6 sc, in ch-3 sp make sc, ch 3 and sc; sc in next 6 sc, skip 2 sc. Repeat from * around. Join and fasten off.

SECOND MOTIF . . . Work as for 1st motif until 9th rnd is completed. **10th rnd:** Skip 1st sc, * sc in next 6 sc, ch 1, sc in corresponding sp on 1st motif, ch 1, sc in next 6 sc, skip 2 sc. Repeat from * once more. Complete 2nd motif same as 1st motif (no more joinings). Fasten off.

Make 16 x 22 motifs, joining them as 2nd motif was joined to 1st, always having one point free between joinings on each motif.

FILL-IN LACE . . . Ch 5. Join with sl st to form ring. **1st rnd:** Ch 1, 16 sc in ring. Join. **2nd rnd:** (Ch 5, skip next sc, sc in next sc) 7 times; ch 2, skip next sc, dc in next sc. **3rd rnd:** (Ch 5, sc in next loop) 7 times; ch 2, dc in next loop. **4th rnd:** Ch 1, * 3 sc in next loop, ch 12, sl st in joining of 2 motifs, ch 12, 3 sc in same loop on Fill-in lace, 3 sc in next loop, ch 5, sl st in ch-3 sp on free point, ch 5, 3 sc in same loop on Fill-in lace. Repeat from * around. Join and fasten off.

Featherspun Filet

MATERIALS:

J. & P. COATS or **CLARK'S O.N.T. BEST SIX CORD MERCERIZED CROCHET,** *Size 30:*

SMALL BALL:

J. & P. COATS —14 balls of White or Ecru, or 18 balls of any color.

OR

CLARK'S O.N.T.—21 balls of White, Ecru, or any color.

BIG BALL:

J. & P. COATS —7 balls of White or Ecru.

Steel Crochet Hook No. 10 or 11.

This amount is sufficient for a centerpiece 14½ inches square, 4 place doilies 12½ inches square, 4 bread and butter plate doilies 8 inches square, and 4 glass doilies 6 inches square.

GAUGE: 5 sps make 1 inch; 5 rows make 1 inch.

CENTERPIECE . . . Starting at bottom of chart, make a chain 18 inches long (16 ch sts to 1 inch). **1st row:** Dc in 8th ch from hook, * ch 2, skip 2 ch, dc in next ch. Repeat from * across until there are 72 sps. Cut off remaining chain. Ch 5, turn. **2nd row:** Dc in next dc (sp over sp made); (ch 2, dc in next dc) 25 times; 2 dc in next sp, dc in next dc (bl over sp made); make 5 more bls, 8 sps, 6 bls, 25 sps, ch 2, skip 2 sts of turning ch, dc in next ch. Ch 5, turn. **3rd row:** Make 25 sps, 1 bl, dc in 18 dc (6 bls over 6 bls made); make 1 more bl, 6 sps, 8 bls, 25 sps. Ch 5, turn. **4th row:** 24 sps, 10 bls, 4 sps, 10 bls, 24 sps. Ch 5, turn. **5th row:** 23 sps, 5 bls, (ch 2, skip 2 dc, dc in next dc) twice (2 sps over 2 bls made); 4 bls, 4 sps, 4 bls, 2 sps, 5 bls, 23 sps. Ch 5, turn. Starting with 6th row, follow chart to top. Do not fasten off, but work sc completely around, keeping work flat. Fasten off.

PLACE DOILY (Make 4) . . . Starting at bottom of chart, make a chain 15 inches long. **1st row:** Work as for 1st row of Centerpiece until there are 62 sps. Cut off remaining chain. Ch 5, turn. Starting with 2nd row, follow chart to top. Do not fasten off but work sc completely around, keeping work flat. Fasten off.

BREAD AND BUTTER PLATE DOILY (Make 4) . . . Starting at bottom of chart, make a chain 10 inches long. **1st row:** Work as for 1st row of Centerpiece until there are 41 sps. Cut off remaining chain. Ch 5, turn. Starting with 2nd row, follow chart to top. Do not fasten off but work sc around, keeping work flat. Fasten off.

GLASS DOILY (Make 4) . . . Starting at bottom of chart, make a chain 8 inches long. **1st row:** Work as for 1st row of Centerpiece until there are 29 sps. Cut off remaining chain. Ch 5, turn. Starting with 2nd row, follow chart to top. Do not fasten off but work sc around, keeping work flat. Fasten off.

Block pieces to measurements given.

PLACE DOILY

START HERE

GLASS DOILY

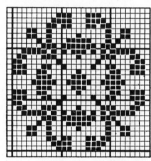

START HERE

WORKING CHARTS FOR FEATHERSPUN FILET SET

CENTERPIECE

START HERE

BREAD AND BUTTER DOILY

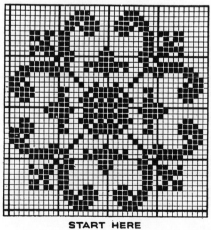

START HERE

There are 10 spaces between heavy lines

Tablecloth measures 66 x 88 inches.

Governor's Lady

MATERIALS:

J. & P. COATS or CLARK'S O.N.T.
BEST SIX CORD MERCERIZED CROCHET, *Size 30:*

SMALL BALL:

J. & P. COATS —85 balls of White or Ecru, or 114 balls of any color
    OR
CLARK'S O.N.T.—136 balls of White, Ecru or any color.

BIG BALL:

J. & P. COATS —43 balls of White or Ecru.

Steel Crochet Hook No. 10 or 11.

GAUGE: Each motif measures 3¼ inches square and 4¼ inches diagonally.

FIRST MOTIF . . . Starting at center, ch 10. Join with sl st to form ring. **1st rnd:** Ch 3 (to count as dc), 23 dc in ring. Join with sl st in top st of starting chain. **2nd rnd:** Ch 6, * skip 1 dc, dc in next dc, ch 3. Repeat from * around, joining last ch-3 with sl st in 3rd st of starting chain. **3rd rnd:** Ch 3, 3 dc in next sp, * dc in next dc, ch 9, (dc in next dc, 3 dc in next sp) twice. Repeat from * around, ending with 3 dc in last sp. Join. **4th rnd:** Ch 3, dc in next 2 dc, * ch 3, 15 dc in next ch-9 loop, ch 3, skip 2 dc, dc in next 5 dc. Repeat from * around, ending with dc in last 2 dc. Join. **5th rnd:** Ch 3, holding back the last loop of each dc on hook make dc in next 2 dc, thread over and draw through all loops on hook (a 2-dc cluster made), * ch 5, sc in next dc, (ch 3, skip 1 dc, sc in next dc) 7 times; ch 5, make a 5-dc cluster over the next 5 dc. Repeat from * around, ending with a 2-dc cluster over the last 2 dc. Join. **6th rnd:** Ch 1, sc in same place as sl st, * ch 7, sc in next ch-3 loop, (ch 3, sc in next loop) 6 times; ch 7, sc in top of next cluster. Repeat from * around, joining last ch-9 with sl st in 1st sc. **7th rnd:** Ch 1, * 9 sc over next loop, sc in next ch-3 loop, (ch 3, sc in next loop) 5 times; 9 sc over next loop. Repeat from * around. Join. **8th rnd:** Sl st in 5 sc, * ch 9, sc in next ch-3 loop, (ch 3, sc in next loop) 4 times; (ch 9, sc in center st of next loop) twice. Repeat from * around, joining last ch-9 with sl st in base of starting chain. **9th rnd:** Ch 1, 11 sc over next loop, * sc in next ch-3 loop, (ch 3, sc in next loop) 3 times; 11 sc over each of next 3 loops. Repeat from * around. Join. **10th rnd:** Sl st in 6 sc, * ch 9, sc in next ch-3 loop, (ch 3, sc in next loop) twice; ch 9, sc in center st of next loop, ch 9, in center st of next loop make tr, ch 15 and tr (corner), ch 9, sc in center st of next loop. Repeat from * around. Join. **11th rnd:** Ch 1, 11 sc over next loop, * sc in next ch-3 loop, ch 3, sc in next ch-3 loop, 11 sc over each of the next 2 loops, 19 sc over corner loop, 11 sc over each of the next 2 loops. Repeat from * around. Join and fasten off.

SECOND MOTIF . . . Work as for 1st motif until 10th rnd is completed. **11th rnd:** Ch 1, 11 sc over next loop, sc in next ch-3 loop, ch 3, sc in next ch-3 loop, 11 sc over each of next 2 loops, 9 sc over corner loop, sc in center st of corresponding corner loop on 1st motif, 9 sc over same corner loop on 2nd motif, (5 sc over next loop, sc in center st on next loop on 1st motif, 5 sc over same loop on 2nd motif) twice; sc in next ch-3 loop, ch 3, sc in next ch-3 loop; work and join next 2 loops same as last 2 loops, then work and join corner loop as before. Complete rnd with no more joinings. Fasten off.

Make all motifs in same way, joining adjacent sides as 2nd motif was joined to 1st (where 4 corners meet, join 3rd and 4th corners to joining of previous 2). Place motifs in the following order: **1st row:** 1 motif. **2nd row:** 3 motifs (one motif extending on each side of previous row). **3rd row:** 5 motifs. **4th row:** 7 motifs. Continue thus, having 2 more motifs on each row until there are 31 motifs on row. Make 5 more rows of 31 motifs each, having 1 motif extend beyond left edge and having 1 motif less on right edge. Now make 2 motifs less on each row (1 motif less on each side) until last row has 1 motif. There are 636 motifs.

Lilac Time

MATERIALS:

J. & P. COATS or CLARK'S O.N.T. BEST SIX CORD MERCERIZED CROCHET, *Size 50:*

J. & P. COATS —9 balls of White or Ecru,
OR
CLARK'S O.N.T.—14 balls of White or Ecru.

Steel Crochet Hook No. 12.   1¼ yards of very fine fabric, 45 inches wide.

GAUGE: 4½ sps make 1 inch; 4½ rows make 1 inch. Tea cloth measures about 49 inches square.

Starting where indicated on chart, ch 67. **1st row:** Tr in 11th ch from hook, tr in next 4 ch, (ch 3, skip 3 ch, tr in next ch) 6 times; tr in next 28 ch. Ch 11, turn. **2nd row:** Tr in 5th ch from hook, tr in next 6 ch, tr in next tr (2 bls increased), ch 3, skip 3 tr, tr in next tr (sp over bl made); (ch 7, skip 7 tr, tr in next tr) 3 times; 3 tr in next sp, tr in next tr (bl over sp made); ch 1, skip 1 ch, tr in next ch, (ch 3, skip 1 ch, tr and 1 ch, tr in next ch) 4 times (4 small honeycombs made); ch 1, tr in next tr, tr in next 4 tr (bl over bl made), ch 3, skip 3 sts of turning ch, tr in next ch (sp over sp made). Ch 7, turn. **3rd row:** Tr in next tr, make 1 bl, 5 small honeycombs, 1 bl, ch 3, skip 3 ch, tr in next ch, (ch 7, tr in center st of next ch-7) twice; ch 7, skip next tr, tr in next tr (3 large honeycombs made); ch 7, make a foundation tr in top st of turning ch as follows: Thread over hook twice, insert hook in top st of turning ch and draw loop through; thread over and draw through 1 loop—*1 ch st made to be used as a foundation st for next tr*—complete tr in usual way—*foundation tr completed.* Make 7 more foundation tr's and 1 more tr in the usual way (2 bls increased). Ch 7, turn. **4th row:** Inc 1 bl, make 3 sps, 1 large honeycomb, 1 sp, tr in next 4 ch, 2 large honeycombs, 1 bl, ch 1, skip 1 ch, tr in next ch, 4 small honeycombs, ch 1, tr in next tr, 1 bl, 1 sp, ch 7, tr in same place as last tr, turn, sl st in 4 ch (1 sp increased). Ch 14, do not turn. **5th row:** Tr in 11th ch from hook, ch 3, tr in same place as last sl st (2 sps increased), make 1 more sp, 1 bl, 1 sp, 1 bl, 3 small honeycombs, 1 bl, 3 large honeycombs, 1 sp, 2 bls, 1 sp, 2 large honeycombs, 1 sp, inc 1 bl. Ch 7, turn.

Now follow chart until 14th row is completed (1 sp decreased at end of 14th row). Turn. **15th row:** Sl st in 3 ch and in next tr (1 sp decreased), ch 7, tr in next tr and follow chart across (1 bl decreased), ch 4, turn. Now follow chart to top of corner finishing scallops individually. Fasten off. Attach thread at "X" and follow chart for other side of lace. Make 8 scallops (between A and B on chart) between corners on all four sides and turn corners as before. When lace is finished sew last row to foundation chain with invisible sts. To even up the inner edge of lace, work as follows: **1st rnd:** Attach thread to 1st of 3 sps at top of any inner scallop, * sl st across top of 3 sps, sc in same place as last sl st, ch 5, sc in next sp, (ch 3, skip next sp, tr in next st) twice; ch 5, sc in next sp, ch 5, holding back the last loop of each tr on hook make tr in next tr, skip next sp, tr in top of tr of next sp, thread over and draw through all loops on hook, ch 5, sc in next sp, ch 5, tr in next tr, ch 4, sl st in corner of next sp, (ch 3, skip 1 sp, tr in next st) 4 times; ch 3, sl st in corner of next sp, work along side of scallop to correspond with opposite side of previous scallop. Repeat from * around, working along inner edges of corners as necessary to even up edge. Join. **2nd rnd:** Work sc closely around. Join and fasten off.

Block lace. Put lace on fabric and baste in place. Sew lace to fabric, cut away excess material and finish raw edges neatly.

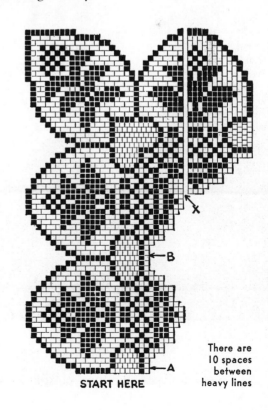

There are 10 spaces between heavy lines

START HERE

45

Inviting as a song at twilight . . . this romantic poppy-patterned tea
cloth whispers the most cordial of welcomes to your unexpected guests.

Tea Cloth

MATERIALS:

CLARK'S BIG BALL MERCERIZED CROCHET,
Size 30:

   3 balls of White or Ecru; or 4 balls of any color.

Steel Crochet Hook No. 10 or 11.

1 yard fabric 36 inches wide.

GAUGE: 5 sps make 1 inch; 5 rows make 1 inch. Lace is made in four individual pieces. Chart given is for one piece.

FIRST SCALLOP . . . Starting at the bottom, ch 24. **1st row:** Dc in 4th ch from hook and in each ch across (22 sts, counting the turning ch). Ch 3, turn. **2nd row:** Dc in next 6 dc (2 bls made), ch 2, skip 2 dc, dc in next dc (sp made over bl), ch 3, skip 2 dc, sc in next dc, ch 3, skip 2 dc, dc in next dc (lacet made). Make 1 sp, then work dc in next 2 dc. Make a foundation dc in top of turning ch as follows: Thread over, insert hook in ch and pull loop through, thread over and draw through 1 loop on hook—*ch st made to be used as a foundation st for next dc;* (thread over and draw through 2 loops) twice—*foundation dc completed.* * Thread over, insert hook in specified ch st and complete another foundation dc as before. Repeat from * 7 more times; then thread over, insert hook in ch at base of last foundation dc made and make 1 dc in usual way (3 bls increased at end of row). Ch 8, turn. **3rd row:** Dc in 4th ch from hook and in next 4 ch, dc in next 4 dc (2 bls increased at beginning of row). Ch 5, skip 5 dc, dc in next dc (bar made), ch 3, skip 2 dc, sc in next dc, ch 3, dc in next dc (another lacet made). Ch 5, dc in next dc (bar made over lacet). Work 1 sp, 2 bls, then ch 3, turn. **4th row:** Dc in next 6 dc, 2 dc in next sp, dc in next dc (bl made over sp), 2 dc over next bar, dc in 3rd st of same bar, ch 2, dc in next dc (bl and sp made over bar). Work 1 bar, then ch 3, skip 2 ch, sc in next ch, ch 3, dc in next dc (lacet made over bar), ch 5, skip 5 dc, dc in next 3 dc, foundation dc in top of turning ch. Work 2 more foundation dc and 1 dc in usual way (1 bl increased at

end of row). Ch 8, turn. Hereafter follow chart from beginning of 5th row and work to 7th row incl. At the end of 7th row, do not fasten off, but lay this piece aside to be worked later.

SECOND SCALLOP . . . Starting at the bottom, ch 45. **1st row:** Dc in 4th ch from hook and in each ch across (43 sts, counting the turning ch). Ch 11, turn. **2nd row:** Dc in 4th ch from hook and in next 7 ch, dc in next 4 dc (3 bls increased at beginning of row). Work 1 sp, (1 lacet, 1 bar) twice; 1 lacet, 1 sp, dc in next 2 dc, foundation dc in top of turning ch. Work 8 more foundation dc and 1 dc in usual way. Ch 8, turn. Hereafter follow chart from beginning of 3rd row and work to 7th row incl. Do not break off, but ch 5, join with sl st to top of turning ch at beginning of 7th row of 1st scallop Fasten off.

THIRD SCALLOP . . . Starting at the bottom, ch 45 and work as before, following chart to 7th row incl. Do not break off, but ch 5, join with sl st to top of turning ch at beginning of 7th row of 2nd scallop. Fasten off. Now ch 3 with ball of thread which remained attached at end of 7th row of 1st scallop, turn and work as follows: **8th row:** 2 bls, 1 sp, 1 lacet, 1 bl, 1 sp, (1 lacet,

(Continued on page 48)

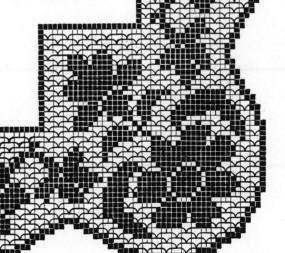

There are 10 spaces between heavy lines

1ST SCALLOP   2ND SCALLOP   3RD SCALLOP

Bread Tray Doily

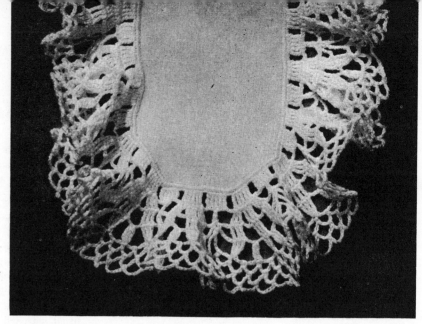

MATERIALS:

CLARK'S O.N.T. "BRILLIANT," 3 balls.

Steel Crochet Hook No. 9.

A piece of linen 3 x 9½ inches.

Tray doily measures 6 x 13½ inches.

Cut corners off linen as in illustration and make a very narrow rolled hem all around. **1st rnd:** Attach thread to one corner of linen, ch 1, 3 sc in same place where thread was attached, then work sc closely over rolled edge, being careful to work 3 sc in same place at each corner. Join with sl st in 1st sc. **2nd rnd:** Ch 4, tr in next 4 sc, * ch 3, skip 2 sc, tr in next 5 sc. Repeat from * around, joining last ch-3 with sl st to top of starting ch-4. There must be an even number of blocks. **3rd rnd:** Ch 4, tr at base of ch-4, * tr in next tr, ch 3, tr in same place, tr in next 2 tr, ch 3, tr in same place, 2 tr in next st, ch 5, skip 2 tr, sc in next st, ch 5, skip 2 tr, work 2 tr in next tr. Repeat from * around. Join. **4th rnd:** Ch 4, tr in next 2 sts, * (ch 5, tr in next 3 tr) twice; ch 5, sc in next 2 loops, ch 5, tr in next 3 tr. Repeat from * around. Join. **5th rnd:**

Ch 4, then holding back the last loop of each tr on hook work tr in next 2 sts, thread over and draw through all loops on hook (cluster made), * ch 5, skip 2 ch, then holding back the last loop of each tr on hook work 3 tr cluster in next ch, ch 5, work 3 tr cluster over next 3 tr, ch 5, skip 2 ch, cluster in next ch, ch 5, cluster over next 3 tr, ch 7, skip 1 sc, sc in next sc, ch 7, cluster over next 3 tr. Repeat from * around. Join. **6th rnd:** Sc in same place as sl st, * (ch 5, sc in next sp, ch 5, sc in top of next cluster) 4 times; (ch 5, sc in next sp) twice; ch 5, sc in top of next cluster. Repeat from * around, ending with ch 2, dc in 1st sc. **7th rnd:** * Ch 6, sc in next loop. Repeat from * around, ending with ch 3, dc in dc. **8th rnd:** * Ch 7, sc in next loop. Repeat from * around, ending with ch 3, tr in dc. Fasten off.

(Continued from page 47)

1 bar) twice; 1 lacet, 1 sp, 1 bl. Work dc in next 5 ch, dc in next dc (2 bls worked over joining ch). Work 1 more bl, 1 sp, (1 lacet, 1 bar) twice; 1 sp, 16 bls, 1 sp, (1 bar, 1 lacet) twice; 1 sp, 1 bl, dc in next 5 ch, 1 bl, 1 sp, 1 lacet, 1 bar, 2 sps, 4 bls, 1 lacet, 1 bar, 7 bls, 1 sp, 4 bls, 1 bar, 1 lacet, 1 bar, 1 bl, inc 1 bl. Ch. 3, turn.

Starting with 9th row, follow chart until 26th row is completed. Ch 3 to turn at end of 26th row. **27th row:** 2 bls, 2 sps, 3 bls, 1 bar, 1 lacet, 1 bar, 1 bl, 1 sp, 1 bar, 2 bls, 1 bar, 1 lacet, (1 sp, 1 bl) twice; 1 bar, 1 lacet, 1 bar, 2 sps, 4 bls, 1 bar, 1 lacet, 1 bar, 1 bl. Ch 3, turn. **28th row:** 1 bl, 1 lacet, 1 bar, 1 lacet, 5 bls, 2 sps, 1 bl, (1 bar, 2 bls) twice; 1 bar, 1 lacet, 3 bls, 1 sp, 1 bar, 2 sps, 1 bar, 4 bls, 1 lacet,

1 sp, 1 bl. Ch 3, turn (1 bl decreased at end of row). **29th and 30th rows:** Follow chart. Do not ch to turn at end of 30th row. **31st row:** Sl st in next 3 sts, ch 3 (1 bl decreased at beginning of row), then work 1 bl, 1 bar, 1 lacet, 10 bls, 1 lacet, 1 bar, 1 sp, 4 bls, 1 bar, 5 bls, 1 sp, 2 bls, 3 sps, 1 bar, 1 lacet, 1 bar, 1 bl. Ch 3, turn. Starting with 32nd row, follow chart to top. Fasten off. This completes 1 piece.

Make 3 more pieces same as this and sew them together with neat over-and-over stitches, being careful to match direction of lacets. In doing this the right and wrong sides of dc rows will not match at seams. Press lace with hot iron through wet cloth. Cut fabric to fit center of lace, making allowance for a narrow hem. Hem fabric and sew to lace.

Pineapples

• So authentically American . . . starry-white pineapple medallions silhouetted against the dark burnished glow of your table top! Easy to do . . . lovely to look at.

MATERIALS:

CLARK'S BIG BALL MERCERIZED CROCHET, *Size 20:*

    4 balls of White or Ecru.

    Steel Crochet Hook No. 8 or 9.

This amount of material is sufficient for a set consisting of a centerpiece about 17½ inches in diameter, 4 place doilies about 14½ inches in diameter, and 4 glass doilies about 6½ inches in diameter.

CENTERPIECE . . . Starting at center, ch 10. Join with sl st to form ring. **1st rnd:** 21 sc in ring. Do not join. **2nd and 3rd rnds:** Sc in each sc around. Sl st in next sc. **4th rnd:** Ch 5, * dc in next sc, ch 2. Repeat from * around, joining last ch-2 with sl st in 3rd st of starting chain (21 sps). **5th rnd:** Sl st in next sp, ch 3, 2 dc in same sp, 3 dc in each sp around. Join with sl st in top st of starting chain. **6th rnd:** Ch 7, * skip 2 dc, dc in next dc, ch 4. Repeat from * around. Join. **7th rnd:** Sl st in next sp, ch 3, 3 dc in same sp, 4 dc in each sp around. Join. **8th rnd:** Ch 8, * skip 3 dc, dc in next dc, ch 5. Repeat from * around. Join. **9th rnd:** Sl st in next

sp, ch 3, in same sp make 2 dc, ch 3 and 3 dc (shell made); in each sp around make a shell of 3 dc, ch 3 and 3 dc. Join.

10th rnd: Sl st in next 2 dc and in sp, ch 3 and complete shell as before (shell over shell made); make shell over shell around. Join. **11th rnd:** Sl st in next 2 dc and in sp, ch 3 and complete shell as before, * ch 1, shell over next shell. Repeat from * around. Join. **12th rnd:** Make shell over shell, having ch 2 (instead of ch-1) between shells. Join. **13th to 17th rnds incl:** Work shell over shell, having 1 ch more between shells on each following rnd (ch 7 on 17th rnd). **18th rnd:** * (Work shell

49

over shell, ch 7) twice; in next shell make 3 dc, ch 5 and 3 dc, **ch 7.** Repeat from * around. Join. **19th rnd:** * (Shell over shell, ch 7) twice; 21 tr in ch-5 sp of next shell (this is base of pineapple), ch 7. Repeat from * around. Join. **20th rnd:** * (Shell over shell, ch 7) twice; sc in each tr, ch 7. Repeat from * around. Join. **21st rnd:** * (Shell over shell, ch 7) twice; sc in next sc, (ch 1, sc in next sc) 20 times; ch 7. Repeat from * around. Join. **22nd rnd:** * (Shell over shell, ch 7) twice; (sc in next ch-1 sp, ch 1) 19 times; ch 7. Repeat from * around. Join. **23rd and 24th rnds:** Same as 22nd rnd, having one ch-1 sp less on each row (17 ch-1 sps on each pineapple). Join.

Now finish each pineapple individually as follows: **1st row:** Sl st in next 2 dc, the following 3 ch and in the next 3 dc, ch 5, turn; work shell over shell, ch 7, make 16 ch-1 sps, ch 7, shell over shell. Ch 5, turn. **2nd row:** Shell over shell, ch 7, make 15 ch-1 sps, ch 7, shell over shell. Ch 5, turn. Now work as for 2nd row, making 1 sp less on each row until 1 sp remains. Ch 5, turn. **Last row:** Shell over shell, ch 7, sc in sp, ch 7, shell over shell, ch 5, turn, sc in sp of last shell, sc in sp of next shell. Fasten off. Attach thread to next free shell and work next pineapple in same way. Complete remaining pineapples. Fasten off. Now work around outer edge of Centerpiece as follows: Attach thread to any ch-5 loop of a point, ch 1, sc in same loop, * in next loop make sc (ch 3, sc in 3rd ch from hook, sc) 3 times; ch 1. Repeat from * to next ch-7 loop, in ch-7 loop make sc, (ch 3, sc in 3rd ch from hook, sc) 5 times; ch 1, sc in next ch-5 loop. Continue thus around. Join and fasten off.

PLACE DOILY (Make 4) . . . Starting at center, ch 8. Join with sl st to form ring. **1st rnd:** 18 sc in ring. Do not join. **2nd, 3rd and 4th rnds:** Same as 2nd, 3rd and 4th rnds of Centerpiece (18 sps).

5th and 6th rnds: Same as 5th and 6th rnds of Centerpiece. **7th, 8th and 9th rnds:** Same as 9th, 11th and 12th rnds of Centerpiece. **10th to 13th rnds incl:** Work shell over shell, having 1 ch more between shells on each following rnd (ch 6 on 13th rnd). **14th rnd:** * (Work shell over shell, ch 6) twice; in next shell make 3 dc, ch 5 and 3 dc, ch 6. Repeat from * around. Join. **15th rnd:** * (Shell over shell, ch 6) twice; 18 tr in ch-5 sp of next shell (base of pineapple), ch 6. Repeat from * around. Join. **16th to 19th rnds incl:** Work as for Centerpiece (20th to 23rd rnds incl), having ch 6 (instead of ch-7) between shells and pineapples, also having ch-1 sps correspond with number of tr at base of pineapple. Now finish each pineapple individually as on Centerpiece. Then work around outer edge same as on Centerpiece. Fasten off.

GLASS DOILY (Make 4) . . . Starting at center, ch 6. Join with sl st to form ring. **1st rnd:** 15 sc in ring. Do not join. **2nd, 3rd and 4th rnds:** Same as 2nd, 3rd and 4th rnds of Centerpiece (15 sps). **5th rnd:** Sl st in next sp, ch 3, in same sp make dc, ch 3 and 2 dc (shell made); in each sp around make a shell of 2 dc, ch 3 and 2 dc (make all shells like this). Join. **6th rnd:** Sl st in next dc and in sp, ch 3 and complete a shell as before, * ch 1, shell over next shell. Repeat from * around. Join. **7th rnd:** Make shell over shell, having ch 2 (instead of ch-1) between shells. Join. **8th rnd:** * (Shell over shell, ch 3) twice; 9 tr in sp of next shell (base of pineapple), ch 3. Repeat from * around. Join. **9th rnd:** * (Shell over shell, ch 3) twice; sc in each tr, ch 3. Repeat from * around. Join. **10th rnd:** * (Shell over shell, ch 3) twice; sc in next sc, (ch 1, sc in next sc) 8 times; ch 3. Repeat from * around. Join.

Now finish each pineapple individually as on Centerpiece. Then work around outer edge to correspond with other doilies, having 1 p between pineapples. Starch lightly and block all pieces to measurements given.

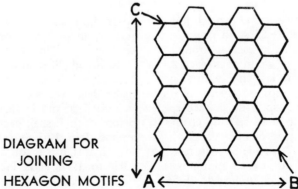

DIAGRAM FOR
JOINING
HEXAGON MOTIFS

Muffin-Cozy

MATERIALS:

J. & P. COATS or CLARK'S O.N.T. BEST SIX CORD MERCERIZED CROCHET, *Size· 30:* 1 ball.

Steel Crochet Hook No. 10 or 11.　　　　A piece of linen, ½ yard square.

Make sure that linen is a true 18-inch square, then cut a 5-inch square out of each corner. You now have a cross-shaped piece of fabric, each arm of which is 8 inches wide and 5 inches long. Shape end of one arm for lace insert as follows: With a pin, mark exact center of end 1½ inches up from edge. Starting at pin, shape scallop as in illustration, leaving 2¼ inches straight at each end. Cut linen along penciled line, then make a very narrow rolled hem all around fabric. **1st row:** Working over rolled edge along shaped end only, attach thread and work sc closely across. Ch 1, turn. **2nd row:** Work ch-5 and sc loops along shaped end, having 10 loops along straight portion of edge, 10 loops along one side of scallop (to center), 10 loops along other side of scallop and 10 loops along remaining straight edge. Fasten off.

INSERT . . . Starting at center, ch 10. Join with sl st to form a ring. **1st rnd:** Ch 1, 20 sc in ring, sl st in 1st sc made. **2nd rnd:** Ch 1, sc in same place as sl st, * ch 5, skip 3 sc, sc in next sc. Repeat from * around. Join last ch-5 with sl st in 1st sc. **3rd rnd:** In each loop around work sc, h dc, 5 dc, h dc and sc. Join. **4th rnd:** * Ch 6, sc between sc's of next 2 petals. Repeat from * around. Join. **5th rnd:** Make a petal in each loop, having 7 dc instead of 5 dc on each petal. **6th rnd:** Same as 4th rnd. **7th rnd:** Sl st into loop, ch 4, 11 tr in same loop, 12 tr in each remaining loop around. Join with sl st to top of ch-4. **8th rnd:** Sc in same place as sl st, * ch 5, skip 3 tr, sc in next tr. Repeat from * around. Join (15 loops). **9th rnd:** Sl st into loop, ch 4, 6 tr in same

loop, * ch 3, (3 sc in next loop) twice; ch 3, 7 tr in next loop. Repeat from * around, joining last ch-3 with sl st in top st of starting chain. **10th rnd:** Sc in same place as sl st, (ch 5, skip 2 tr, sc in next tr) twice; 3 sc in loop, sc in next 6 sc, 3 sc in next loop, sc in next tr, ch 2, then pick up linen and, holding shaped edge so that loops face toward you, work sc in 16th loop from right-hand end (thus joining). Ch 2, skip 2 tr on insert, sc in next tr, ch 2, sc in next loop on linen, ch 2, skip 2 tr, sc in next tr, 3 sc in loop, sc in next 6 sc, 3 sc in next loop, sc in next tr, ch 2, skip 6 loops on linen, sc in next loop, ch 2, skip 2 tr, sc in next tr. Join next loop as before, then continue in pattern around insert (no more joinings). Join and fasten off.

EDGING . . . 1st row: Working along shaped end and with right side facing, attach thread to 1st sc. Work 3 sc in ch-5 loop, ch 5, make a 3-d tr cluster as follows: Holding back the last loop of each d tr on hook, work 3 d tr in same ch-5 loop where sc's were made, thread over and draw through all loops on hook. (Ch 7, sc in next loop, ch 5, sc in next loop, ch 7, 3-d tr cluster in next loop) 3 times; ch 7, sc in next loop, ch 5, sc in next loop, (3-d tr cluster in next free loop on insert, ch 6, 3-d tr cluster in same loop, ch 6) twice; (in next loop work 3-d tr clusters with ch 6 between, and ch 6) twice. Continue to work to correspond with first half, ending with 4-d tr cluster in last loop. Ch 1, turn. **2nd row:** Sc under ch-7, then * ch 6, (sc under next ch-7) twice. Repeat from * 2 more times; skip 2 loops, work 5 sc in next loop, (7 sc in next loop) 9 times;

(continued on next page)

5 sc in next loop, skip 2 loops, * * (sc under next ch-7) twice; ch 6. Repeat from * * 2 more times; sc under next ch-7. Fasten off. **3rd row:** With right side facing attach thread to 3rd sc of 1st row and work as follows: Make 6 sc under the ch-5, then ch 7, turn, work sc in same place where thread was attached, turn, in ch-7 loop work (3 sc, ch 3) twice, and 3 sc; then work 3 sc under same ch-5 where 7 sc were worked, sc in tip of cluster, 3 sc in ch-6 loop, ch 7, turn, skip 6 sc, sc in next sc, turn, in ch-7 loop work (3 sc, ch 3) twice, and 3 sc; then * work 6 sc in same ch-6 loop where 3 sc were worked, sc between next 2 sc, 3 sc in next loop, ch 7,

turn, complete scallop as before. Repeat from * once more, work 6 sc in same ch-6 loop, sc in next 4 sc, ch 7, turn, complete scallop as before, (sc in next 10 sc, ch 7, turn, complete scallop as before) twice; (sc in next 9 sc, ch 7, turn, complete scallop) 4 times; sc in next 10 sc, ch 7, turn, complete scallop, sc in next 7 sc, 3 sc in next loop, ch 7, turn, complete scallop and work to corner to correspond with first half. Work a scallop at side of edging, 3 sc in next loop, then, working over rolled edge of linen, work 7 sc in edge, * * ch 7, turn, complete scallop as before, work 10 sc in edge. Repeat from * * around remainder of linen. Join and fasten off.

Dewdrop Doily

MATERIALS:

J. & P. COATS or CLARK'S O.N.T. BEST SIX CORD MERCERIZED CROCHET, *Size 20:*

1 ball of White or Ecru for set of 4 doilies.

Steel Crochet Hook No. 8 or 9.

Doily measures about 4½ inches in diameter.

Starting at center, ch 8. Join with sl st to form ring. **1st rnd:** Ch 5, (dc in ring, ch 2) 11 times. Join last ch-2 with sl st in top st of starting chain. **2nd rnd:** Ch 4, * 3 tr in next sp, tr in next dc. Repeat from * around, ending with 3 tr in last sp; join. **3rd rnd:** Ch 1, sc in same place as sl st, * ch 5, skip next tr, sc in next tr. Repeat from * around, ending with ch 2, dc in 1st sc made. **4th rnd:** * Ch 5, sc in next loop. Repeat from * around, ending with ch 2, dc in dc of 3rd rnd. **5th rnd:** * Ch 10, skip 1 loop, sc in next loop. Repeat from * around, joining last ch-10 with sl st in dc of 4th rnd. **6th rnd:** In each ch-10 make 6 sc, ch 5 and 6 sc. **7th rnd:** Sl st in 6 sc, sl st in loop, ch 4 (to count as tr), holding back the last loop of each tr on hook make tr in same loop, thread over and draw through all loops on hook (a 3-tr cluster made), * (ch 7, 3-tr cluster in same loop) twice; 3-tr cluster in next loop. Repeat from * around, joining last cluster with sl st in top of 1st cluster. **8th rnd:** Sl st in 3 ch, ch 1, sc in same loop, * ch 10, sc in next loop. Repeat from * around, joining last ch-10 with sl st in 1st sc made. Fasten off. Starch lightly and block to measurement.

Stardust Doily

MATERIALS:

CLARK'S BIG BALL MERCERIZED CROCHET, *Size 20:*

1 ball of White or Ecru for a set of 12 doilies.

Steel Crochet Hook No. 8 or 9.

Each doily measures about 5 inches in diameter.

Starting at center, ch 8. Join with sl st to form ring. **1st rnd:** Ch 3, 23 dc in ring. Sl st in top st of ch-3. **2nd rnd:** Ch 3, dc in next 2 dc, * ch 3, dc in next 3 dc. Repeat from * around, ending with ch 3. Join. **3rd rnd:** Sl st in next 2 dc, ch 4 (to count as tr), holding back the last loop of each tr on hook make 3 tr in next sp and 1 tr in next dc, thread over and draw through all loops on hook (5-tr cluster made), * ch 8, holding back the last loop of each tr on hook make tr in last dc of this 3-dc group, 3 tr in next sp and tr in 1st dc of next dc-group, thread over and complete cluster as before. Repeat from * around, joining last ch-8 with sl st in tip of 1st cluster made. **4th rnd:** 9 sc in each sp around. Join. **5th rnd:** Ch 1, sc in same place as sl st, * ch 7, skip 2 sc, make a 3-tr cluster in next sc, ch 13, dc in 13th ch from hook, skip 2 sc, 3-tr cluster in next sc, ch 7, skip 2 sc, sc in next sc. Repeat from * around. Join last ch-7 with sl st in 1st sc. **6th rnd:** Sl st in next 3 ch, sc in loop, ch 4, * make a 3-tr cluster in ch-13 loop, (ch 10, dc in 10th ch from hook, another 3-tr cluster in same ch-13 loop) 6 times; (tr in next ch-7 loop) twice. Repeat from * around, ending with tr in last ch-7 loop, sl st in top st of ch-4. Fasten off. Starch lightly and block to measurement.

Crocheted Accessories for Your Home

• For festive entertaining, small buffet suppers . . . or little dinners à deux . . . there's nothing on earth more stunning with the twinkle of goblets and the stardust of crystal . . . than gossamer glamour like this crochet!

↑ DEWDROP DOILY
    . . . This doily measures 4½ inches in diameter.

STARDUST DOILY   →
    . . . This doily measures 5 inches in diameter.

Peasant Polka

MATERIALS:

J. & P. COATS KNIT-CRO-SHEEN,
7 balls of Light and 9 balls of Dark.

Steel Crochet Hook No. 5.

The above amount of material is sufficient for 4 place mats,
each 10½ x 16 inches, and a runner of the same size.

GAUGE: Each motif measures 1⅞ inches in diameter. **Use thread double throughout.**

PLACE MAT (Make 4) . . . Motif: 1st rnd: Starting at center with Light, ch 4, work 15 dc in 1st ch made. Sl st in top st of starting chain. **2nd rnd:** Ch 3, dc in same place as sl st, 2 dc in each dc around (32 dc). Join and fasten off. **3rd rnd:** Attach Dark at joining and work sc in each st around. Do not join, but make sc's all around, working sc's in base of sc's of previous rnd. Join and fasten off.

Make 43 more motifs exactly like this. Now make 10 motifs using only Dark. Arrange Dark motifs in 2 rows of 5 motifs each. Join them by sewing the outside loop of 3 corresponding sts together. Now sew 2 rows of two-color motifs around this Dark center. Make 5 pieces; use one for a runner.

TABLE FOR TWO

MATERIALS:

J. & P. COATS KNIT-CRO-SHEEN, 10 balls of White or Ecru, or 16 balls of any color.

OR

CLARK'S O.N.T. LUSTERSHEEN, 10 skeins of White or Ecru, or 13 skeins of any color.

MILWARD'S Steel Crochet Hook No. 7.

GAUGE . . . 3 sps make 1¼ inches; 3 rows make 1¼ inches. Each block measures about 17 inches square. For a tablecloth about 54 inches square, make 3 x 3 blocks.

BLOCK . . . Starting at center, ch 13 and make tr in 13th ch from hook. **1st rnd:** (Ch 7, tr in same place as last tr) twice. Ch 3, skip 3 ch, tr in next ch, ch 7, tr in same place as last tr, ch 3, skip 3 ch, tr in next ch, ch 7, tr in same place as last tr, ch 3, tr in next tr, ch 3, skip 3 ch, tr in next ch. **2nd rnd:** Ch 11, tr in top of last tr, ch 3, tr at base of same tr, tr in next 3 ch, tr in next tr, ch 3. Skip 3 ch, * into next ch make tr, ch 7 and tr; ch 3, tr in next tr, tr in next 3 ch, tr in tr, ch 3, skip 3 ch. Repeat from * around, ending with ch 3; sl st in 4th st of ch-11. **3rd rnd:** Ch 4, tr in next 4 ch, * ch 7, tr in same place as last tr, tr in next 3 ch, tr in tr, tr in next 3 ch, tr in next tr *(2 bls made)*; ch 3, skip 3 tr, tr in next tr *(1 sp made)*. Make 2 bls. Repeat from * around, ending with tr in next 3 ch, sl st in 4th ch of ch-4.

4th rnd: Ch 4, tr in next 4 tr, tr in next 4 ch, * ch 7, tr in same place as last tr, 2 bls, 3 sps, 2 bls.

Repeat from * around, ending with ch 3, sl st in 4th ch of ch-4. Starting at 5th rnd, follow chart until block is completed (the first sp of 5th rnd is indicated by "X" on chart). Make 3 x 3 blocks. Sew blocks together on wrong side with neat over-and-over stitches.

EDGING . . . 1st rnd: Attach thread to one tr, ch 4 and work tr in each tr, and 3 tr in each sp around, making 4 tr, ch 7 and 4 tr at corners of cloth. Join with sl st. **2nd and 3rd rnds:** Ch 4, tr in each tr around, making 4 tr, ch 7 and 4 tr in each corner. Fasten off.

DOTS INDICATE CORNER SPACES

PENTHOUSE

Up-to-the-minute as the New York skyline, and as exciting, with its dynamic pattern built of sheer and solid blocks etched on mesh! Made with today's speed . . . crochet a block a day for twelve days and it's all done!

MATERIALS:

J. & P. COATS KNIT-CRO-SHEEN, 18 balls of White or Ecru, or 29 balls of any color.

OR

CLARK'S O.N.T. LUSTERSHEEN, 18 skeins of White or Ecru, or 24 skeins of any color.

MILWARD'S Steel Crochet Hook No. 7.

GAUGE . . . 6 sps make 2¼ inches; 6 rows make 2¼ inches. Each block measures about 21½ inches square, before blocking. Completed tablecloth measures about 73 x 97 inches.

BLOCK . . . Starting at center, ch 8, tr in 5th ch from hook, tr in next 3 ch. Work is now done in rounds.
1st rnd: Ch 7 (to count as tr and ch-3); in same place as last tr make tr, ch 7 and tr. Ch 3, skip 3 tr, tr

at base of turning ch, ch 7, tr in same place as last tr. Ch 3, tr at top of turning ch, ch 7, tr in same place as last tr, ch 3, skip 3 tr, tr in next tr, ch 3, join with tr in 4th ch of ch-7 first made (8 sps in rnd).

2nd rnd: Ch 4, 3 tr over bar of last tr, tr at base of same tr—*1 bl made.* * Ch 1, skip 1 ch, tr in next ch; ch 1, skip 1 ch, tr in next tr—*a shadow sp made.* Make 3 tr over next ch, tr in 4th st of same ch—*another bl made.* Ch 7, tr in same place as last tr, 3 tr over same ch, tr in next tr. Repeat from * 2 more times, ch 1, skip 1 ch, tr in next ch, ch 1, tr in next tr, 3 tr over next ch, tr in top of joining tr of previous rnd, ch 3, join with tr in 4th st of ch-4 first made.

3rd rnd: Ch 4, 3 tr over bar of last tr, tr at base of same tr, tr in next 4 tr—*bl over bl.* * (Ch 1, tr in next tr) twice—*shadow sp made over shadow sp.* Make tr in next 4 tr, 3 tr over next ch, tr in 4th st of same

□ SP.   ■ BL.   ◪ SHADOW SP.

56

ch, ch 7, tr in same place as last tr, 3 tr over same ch, tr in next 5 tr. Repeat from * 2 more times, (ch 1, tr in next tr) twice; tr in next 4 tr, 3 tr over next ch, tr in top of joining tr of previous rnd, ch 3, join with tr in 4th st of ch-4 first made.

Starting with 4th rnd, follow chart until 6th rnd is completed. **7th rnd:** Ch 5 (to count as tr and ch-1), tr in center of bar of last tr, ch 1, tr at base of same tr. * (Ch 1, skip 1 tr, tr in next tr) 10 times—*5 shadow sps made over 5 bls.* Make shadow sp over shadow sp, shadow sp over next 5 bls; (ch 1, skip 1 ch, tr in next ch) twice. Ch 7, tr in same place as last tr, ch 1, skip 1 ch, tr in next ch, ch 1, tr in next tr. Repeat from * around, ending with ch 3, tr in 4th ch of ch-5 first made.

8th rnd: Ch 4, 3 tr over bar of last tr, tr at base of same tr. * Shadow sp over shadow sp; (tr in next ch, tr in next tr) 8 times—*4 bls made over 4 shadow sps.* Make shadow sp over next 3 shadow sps, 4 bls, 1 shadow sp, 3 tr over next ch, tr in 4th st of same ch, ch 7, tr in same place as last tr, 3 tr over same ch, tr in

next tr. Repeat from * around, ending with ch 3, tr in 4th st of ch-4 first made. Starting with 9th rnd, follow chart until block is completed. Fasten off.

Make 3 x 4 blocks, and ·sew blocks together on wrong side with neat over-and-over stitches.

EDGING . . . 1st rnd: Attach thread to one tr, ch 4 and work tr in each tr, tr in each ch-1, and 3 tr in each space all around, making 4 tr, ch 7 and 4 tr at corners. Join with sl st to top of ch-4 first made. **2nd rnd:** Ch 5 (to count as tr and ch-1), skip 1 tr, * tr in next tr, ch 1, skip 1 tr. Repeat from * to corner ch-7. Over ch-7, make (ch 1, skip 1 ch, tr in next ch) twice, ch 7, tr in same place as last tr, (ch 1, skip 1 ch, tr in next st) twice. Work around and join with sl st to 4th ch of ch-5 first made. **3rd rnd:** Ch 4, tr in each tr and each ch-1 around, making 4 tr, ch 7 and 4 tr in corners. Fasten off.

Block to measure 73 x 97 inches.

SPANISH INFANTA

Remember the wonderful old paintings of Spanish court beauties in their gorgeous lace mantillas? With its breath-taking beauty, this cloth borrows the fabulous quality of that famous lace . . . a delicate, diaphanous texture that brings out the sparkle of your china . . . the sheen of your silver! Exquisitely lacy and open, it's a proud jewel for your table . . . a treasure to reveal memorably!

MATERIALS:

CLARK'S O.N.T. or J. & P. COATS BIG BALL BEST SIX CORD MERCERIZED CROCHET, size 20, 29 balls of White or Ecru.

MILWARD'S Steel Crochet Hook No. 9 or 10.

GAUGE . . . Each motif measures 4½ inches in diameter (from point to point) before blocking. Finished tablecloth measures about 72 x 90 inches, and requires 15 x 19 motifs.

FIRST MOTIF . . . Starting at center, ch 10, join with sl st. **1st rnd:** Ch 3, 23 d c in ring. Join with sl st to 3rd st of ch-3 at beginning of rnd. **2nd rnd:** (Ch 5, skip 1 d c, s c in next d c) 11 times; ch 2, d c in same place as sl st (on previous rnd). **3rd rnd:** (Ch 5, s c in next loop) 11 times; ch 2, d c in tip of d c of previous rnd. **4th rnd:** Same as 3rd rnd, but end with ch-5, sl st in tip of d c.

   5th rnd: Ch 4, 3 tr in d c where sl st was made, holding back the last loop of each tr on hook; thread over and draw through all loops on hook, ch 1 to fasten *(thus making a 3-tr cluster).* * Ch 5, s c in next loop, ch 5, 4 tr in next s c, holding back the last loop of each tr on hook; thread over and draw through all loops on hook, ch 1 to fasten *(thus making a 4-tr cluster).* Repeat from * around, ending with s c in last loop, ch 5, sl st to tip of first cluster. **6th rnd:** S c in same place as sl st, * ch 7, s c in tip of next cluster. Repeat from * around. Join last ch-7 with sl st to first s c. **7th rnd:** Ch 4, 3-tr cluster in same place as sl st, * ch 6, s c in next ch-7 loop, ch 6, 4-tr cluster in next s c. Repeat from * around, ending with ch-6, sl st to tip of first cluster.

   8th rnd: Ch 8 (to count as tr and ch-4); in same place as sl st make d c, ch 4 and tr. * Ch 4, in tip of next cluster make tr, ch 4, d c, ch 4 and tr. Repeat from * around, ending with ch-4, sl st in 4th st of ch-8. **9th rnd:** S c in same place as sl st, * ch 4, in next d c make d c, ch 3 and d c; ch 4, s c in next tr, 4 s c in next ch-4 sp, s c in next tr. Repeat from * around, ending with 4 s c in last ch-4 sp, sl st in s c at base of ch-4 made at beginning of rnd. **10th rnd:** * 4 s c in next ch-4 sp; in next ch-3 sp make s c, half d c, d c, ch 3, d c, half d c and s c; 4 s c in next ch-4 sp, s c in next 6 s c. Repeat from * around; join with sl st to 1st s c made. Break off. This completes first motif.

SECOND MOTIF . . . Work 1st 9 rnds of first motif. **10th rnd:** * 4 s c in next ch-4 sp; in next ch-3 sp make s c, half d c, d c, ch 1, sl st in a point of first motif, ch 1. Make d c, half d c, and s c in same ch-3 on second motif as last d c was made; 4 s c in next ch-4 sp, s c in next 6 s c. Repeat from * once more. Complete rnd as for first motif (do not make any more joinings).

   Make 15 x 19 motifs, joining 2 points of each motif to 2 points of adjacent motifs, leaving one point free between joinings on each motif, for fill-in lace to be worked later.

FILL-IN LACE . . . Starting at center, ch 10, join with sl st. **1st rnd:** Ch 3, 23 d c in ring. Join to 3rd st of ch-3. **2nd rnd:** * Ch 7, sl st in free point between joinings, ch 7, skip 2 d c on ring, s c in next d c, ch 12, sl st in joining, ch 12, skip 2 d c on ring, s c in next d c. Repeat from * around, ending with ch 12, skip 2 d c on ring, s c at base of ch-7 first made. Fasten off. Fill in all spaces between joinings in this manner.

Block to measure 72 x 90 inches.

HORN OF PLENTY

A cloth with subtle distinction. Note the repeating Maltese cross design both in the openwork of the square and in the fascinating way the squares are joined with one another. It is unusual and unusually lovely, and if you wish to treat yourself to an out-of-the-ordinary cloth that has both dignity and beauty, you'll adore the subtle flattery of this table setting.

MATERIALS:

CLARK'S BIG BALL MERCERIZED CROCHET,
size 20, 19 balls of White or Ecru.

MILWARD'S Steel Crochet Hook No. 8 or 9.

GAUGE . . . Motif measures about 3½ inches square before blocking. For a tablecloth 54 x 72 inches, make 15 x 20 motifs.

FIRST MOTIF . . . 1st rnd: * Ch 12, join with sl st to 1st ch of ch-12, 6 s c in ch-12. Repeat from * 3 more times. Drop loop from hook and, holding work so that all s c's are right side up, insert hook in ch preceding 1st s c made and draw dropped loop through (thus forming a large ring, with all s c's at center). **2nd rnd:** * In center sp between s c-groups make s c, ch 3 and s c; 7 s c in next ch-12. Repeat from * around; join to 1st s c made.

3rd rnd: Sl st in·ch-3 loop, ch 4 (to count as tr); make 2 tr in same loop, retaining on hook last loop of each tr; thread over and draw through all loops (a tr-cluster made). * Ch 3 more; make 3 tr in same ch-3 loop, retaining on hook last loop of each tr, and complete cluster; ch 3, another cluster in same loop. Ch 5, 3-tr cluster in next ch-3 loop. Repeat from * around, joining last ch-5 to tip of 1st cluster. **4th rnd:** Ch 3 (to count as d c), * 6 d c in next ch-3 sp; in tip of next cluster make d c, ch 3 and d c; 6 d c in next ch-3 sp, d c in tip of next cluster, ch 4, d c in tip of next cluster. Repeat from * around, joining last ch-4 to top of ch-3.

5th rnd: Sl st in next d c, ch 3 (to count as d c), d c in next 5 d c, * ch 3, skip 1 d c, in corner ch-3 make 3-tr cluster, ch 3 and another 3-tr cluster. Ch 3, skip 1 d c, d c in next 6 d c, ch 5, skip ch-4 and 1st d c of next d c-group, d c in next 6 d c. Repeat from * around, joining last ch-5 to top of ch-3. **6th rnd:** Sl st in next d c, ch 3, d c in next 3 d c; * ch 3, 3-d c cluster in next ch-3 sp—*to make 3-d c cluster, make 3 d c, retaining on hook last loop of each st; thread over and complete as for previous clusters.* Ch 3, in corner ch-3 make 3-d c cluster, ch 3 and a 3-d c cluster. Ch 3, 3-d c cluster in next ch-3, ch 3, skip 1 d c, d c in next 4 d c, ch 3, d c in 3rd st of ch-5, ch 3, skip 1 d c of next group, d c in next 4 d c. Repeat from * around, joining last ch-3 to 1st ch-3.

7th rnd: Sl st in next d c, ch 3, d c in next d c; * (ch 3, in next sp make a 3-d c cluster) twice. Ch 3, in corner ch-3 sp make a 3-d c cluster, ch 3 and another 3-d c cluster. (Ch 3, 3-d c cluster in next sp) twice; ch 3, skip 1 d c of 4-d c group, d c in next 2 d c, ch 4, skip 1 d c and the ch-3 below, d c in next d c, ch 4, skip ch-3 and 1 d c, d c in next 2 d c. Repeat from * around, ending with ch 4; join.

8th rnd: Ch 3, d c in next d c, * (2 d c in sp, d c in tip of cluster) 3 times; in corner sp make 3 d c, ch 3 and 3 d c. D c in cluster; (2 d c in sp, d c in

cluster) twice; 2 d c in sp, d c in next 2 d c, 4 d c in ch-4 sp, d c in d c, 4 d c in ch-4 sp, d c in 2 d c. Repeat from * around, ending with 4 d c; join. **9th rnd:** * Ch 5, skip 3 d c, s c in next d c, ch 5, skip 2 d c, s c in next d c, ch 5, skip 3 d c, s c in next d c. Ch 5, in corner sp make s c, ch 4 and s c. Now continue making ch-5 loops along all sides, skipping 2 d c for one loop and 3 d c for the next loop alternately, and making s c, ch 4 and s c in each corner sp. Fasten off. This completes one motif.

SECOND MOTIF . . . Work 1st 8 rnds as for first motif. **9th rnd:** Work as for 1st motif to s c, ch-4 and s c, inclusive, of 1st corner. Then ch 5, skip 2 d c, s c in next d c, ch 2, sl st in center ch of 2nd loop following corner on 1st motif, ch 2, skip 3 d c on motif in work, s c in next d c. Continue joining loops as before until 9 loops are joined. Complete rnd as for 1st motif (no more joinings).

Make 15 x 20 motifs, joining each motif to adjacent motifs, as second was joined to first. Block to measure 54 x 72 inches.

ONE O'CLOCK

Crocheted place mats are smart . . . so pretty on a highly polished table top and such a joy to do up. Centering each square motif is a lacy flower of Spring-like daintiness . . . the square frame makes a smart all-over pattern. Small motifs are so handy to make, for you can carry your crochet hook and a ball of Clark's O.N.T. or J. & P. Coats crochet thread and whip up several motifs in no time at all!

MATERIALS:

CLARK'S O.N.T. or J. & P. COATS BIG BALL BEST SIX CORD MERCERIZED CROCHET, size 30:

CLARK'S O.N.T.—7 balls of White or Ecru.

J. & P. COATS—7 balls of White or Ecru, or 10 balls of any color.

MILWARD'S Steel Crochet Hook No. 11.

The above materials are sufficient for a luncheon set consisting of 4 place mats, each 10½ x 17 inches; and a center mat 14 x 28 inches.

GAUGE . . . Each motif measures 3¼ inches square before blocking.

PLACE MATS (Make 4)—FIRST MOTIF . . . 1st rnd: Starting at center, * ch 5, 2 tr in 5th ch from hook, holding back the last loop of each tr on hook; thread over and draw through all 3 loops on hook, ch 1 to fasten (*a cluster made*). Ch 4, sl st in tip of cluster (*a p made*), ch 4, sl st in base of cluster. Repeat from * 7 more times. Join with sl st to base of 1st cluster. **2nd rnd:** Ch 6, remove hook, place last ch-6 at back of work, insert hook in p at tip of 1st cluster and draw dropped loop through. Ch 3, 8 d c in same p (a shell made). Make 9 d c in p at tip of next 7 clusters. Join with sl st to 3rd ch of ch-3.

3rd rnd: * S c in next d c, (ch 4, skip 1 d c, s c in next d c) 3 times. Ch 1, skip last d c of this shell and 1 d c of next shell. Repeat from * around. Join last ch-1 to 1st s c made. **4th rnd:** Sl st to center of next loop, s c in same loop, * ch 3, in next loop make (d c, ch 4, sl st in 4th ch from hook—*a p made*—ch 1) 3 times. D c in same loop, ch 3, s c in next loop, ch 2, skip ch-1 sp, s c in next loop. Repeat from *

around. Join last ch-2 to 1st s c made. Fasten off. **5th rnd:** Attach thread and make s c in center p above one shell, * ch 12, d tr in center p above next shell, ch 15, d tr in same p (this is corner). Ch 12, s c in center p above next shell. Repeat from * around. Join to 1st s c.

6th rnd: Ch 6, skip 3 sts, d c in next st, (ch 3, skip 3 sts, d c in next st) 4 times. * Ch 3, tr in next st, ch 3, d c in next st—*corner*. (Ch 3, skip 3 sts, d c in next st) 10 times. Repeat from * around. Join last ch-3 to 3rd st of ch-6. **7th rnd:** * In next sp make half d c and 2 d c. In next d c make tr, ch-4 p and tr. In next sp make 2 d c and half d c. Skip next d c. Repeat from * 2 more times. In tr make d c, 2 tr, p, 2 tr and d c (corner). In next sp make half d c, and 2 d c. In next d c make tr, p and tr. In next sp make 2 d c and half d c. Continue in this manner around, working other corners as for first corner. Join and fasten off.

SECOND MOTIF . . . Work first 6 rnds as for first motif. **7th rnd:** * In next sp make half d c and 2 d c. In next d c make tr, ch-4 p and tr. In next sp make 2 d c and half d c; skip next d c. Repeat from * 2 more times. In tr make d c, 2 tr, ch 2, sl st in corner p of first motif, ch 2, 2 tr back in same place as last 2 tr on second motif. Continue as for 7th rnd of first motif, joining next 7 p's to adjacent p's of first motif as previous p was joined (no more joinings). Complete as for first motif.

Make 3 x 5 motifs, joining motifs as second was joined to first (where 4 corners meet, join 3rd and 4th corners to joining of other corners).

CENTER MAT . . . Make 4 x 8 motifs, joining as for place mats. Block pieces to measurements given.

NEW LOVE

For simple dignity and gracious formality, choose a pristine filet cloth like this beauty, where a stylized flower, grown to giant size like a lush tropical bloom, shows a subtle play of light and shadow in its composition. Made in large squares (thirty in all) for this grand size cloth.

MATERIALS:

CLARK'S O.N.T. or J. & P. COATS BIG BALL BEST SIX CORD MERCERIZED CROCHET, size 50, 35 balls of White or Ecru.

MILWARD'S Steel Crochet Hook No. 12.

GAUGE . . . 9 sps make 2 inches; 9 rows make 2 inches. Completed block measures about 15 inches square. For a tablecloth 75 x 90 inches, make 5 x 6 blocks.

BLOCK . . . Starting at bottom of chart, make a chain about 20 inches long (18 ch sts to 1 inch). **1st row:** Tr in 5th ch from hook and in next 7 ch (9 tr, counting turning ch). Then (ch 1, skip 1 ch, tr in next ch) twice—*a shadow sp made.* Make another shadow sp,

make tr in next 8 ch—*2 bls made;* (2 shadow sps, 2 bls) 6 times; 2 shadow sps, tr in next 16 ch—*4 bls made;* (2 shadow sps, 2 bls) 8 times. Cut off remaining chain. Ch 4, turn.

2nd row: Tr in next 4 tr—*a bl made.* (Ch 1, skip 1 tr, tr in next tr) twice—*a shadow sp over a bl.* (Tr in next ch, tr in next tr) 4 times—*2 bls made over 2 shadow sps.* Make (2 shadow sps, 2 bls) 7 times; 4 shadow sps, (2 bls, 2 shadow sps) 7 times; 2 bls, 1 shadow sp, 1 bl. Ch 5 *to count as tr and ch-1,* turn.
3rd row: Skip 1 tr, tr in next tr, ch 1, skip 1 tr, tr in next tr *(a shadow sp made at beginning of row),* 1 bl, 64 shadow sps, 1 bl, 1 shadow sp. Ch 5, turn.
4th row: Same as 3rd row. Ch 4, turn. **5th row:** 1 bl, 8 shadow sps, ch 3, skip next tr, make tr in next tr—*1 sp made over a shadow sp.* Make 49 more sps, 8 shadow sps, 1 bl. Ch 4, turn.

6th row: 1 bl, 8 shadow sps, ch 1, skip 1 ch, tr in next ch, ch 1, skip 1 ch, tr in next tr—*shadow sp made over a sp.* Make 2 more shadow sps, ch 3, tr in next tr—*sp made over sp.* Make 43 more sps, 11 shadow sps, 1 bl. Ch 5, turn.
7th row: 1 shadow sp, 1 bl, 10 shadow sps, 44 sps, 10 shadow sps, 1 bl, 1 shadow sp. Now follow chart to top, starting at 8th row. Fasten off.

This completes one block. Make 5 x 6 blocks and sew together on wrong side with neat over-and-over stitches. Block cloth to measure 75 x 90 inches.

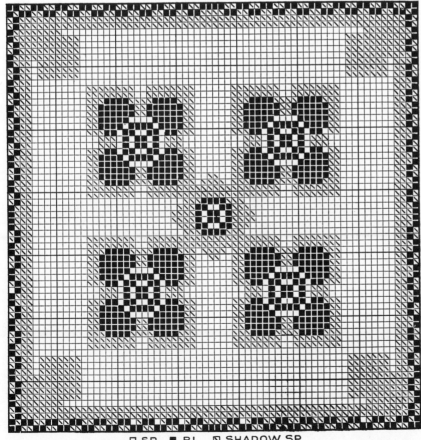

□ SP   ■ BL   ◩ SHADOW SP
THERE ARE TEN SPACES BETWEEN HEAVY LINES

LADY BOUNTIFUL

Lady Bountiful has a grandeur and chic about it, for each round motif bursts with the splendid flamboyant beauty of a sunflower! Since people just naturally drift to your house, and because you're so proud of your table appointments, you'll adore this cloth . . . for it gives whatever you serve an important air, and will make yours one of the most hospitable tables in town.

MATERIALS:
CLARK'S BIG BALL MERCERIZED CROCHET, size 20, 24 balls of White or Ecru.
MILWARD'S Steel Crochet Hook No. 8 or 9.

GAUGE . . . Each motif measures about 4½ inches in diameter, before blocking. For a tablecloth about 60 x 80 inches, make 13 x 17 motifs.

FIRST MOTIF . . . Starting at center, ch 8, join with sl st. **1st rnd:** Ch 5, (tr in ring, ch 1) 15 times. Join to 4th ch of ch-5. **2nd rnd:** Sl st in next sp, ch 7; (tr in next ch-1 sp, ch 3) 15 times. Join to 4th ch of ch-7. **3rd rnd:** S c in next sp, ch 4, 3 tr in same sp, holding back the last loop of each tr on hook; thread over and draw through all loops on hook, ch 1 to fasten (a cluster). * Ch 4, 4 tr in next sp, holding back the last loop of each tr on hook; finish as for a cluster. Repeat from * around. Join last ch-4 to tip of first cluster.

4th rnd: Ch 6, * s c in next sp, ch 3, d c in tip of next cluster, ch 3. Repeat from * around; join last ch-3 to 3rd ch of ch-6. **5th rnd:** Ch 10, * d c in next d c, ch 7. Repeat from * around. Join last ch-7 to 3rd ch of ch-10. **6th rnd:** Ch 6, tr in same place as sl st, * 7 d c in next ch-7 sp, in next d c make tr, ch 2 and tr. Repeat from * around; sl st in 4th ch of ch-6. **7th rnd:** Sl st in next sp, ch 6, d c in same sp, * ch 3, s c in 4th d c of 7-d c group, ch 3. In next ch-2 sp make d c, ch 3 and d c. Repeat from * around. Join last ch-3 with sl st to 3rd ch of ch-6.

8th rnd: Sl st in next sp, ch 5; in same place as sl st make d c, ch 2, d c, ch 2 and d c. * Ch 3, s c in next s c, ch 3. In next sp between 2 d c make (d c, ch 2) 3 times and d c. Repeat from * around. Join last ch-3 to 3rd ch of ch-5. Fasten off.

SECOND MOTIF . . . Work first 7 rnds as for first motif. **8th rnd:** Sl st in next sp, ch 5, d c in same place as sl st, ch 1, sl st in corresponding sp of first motif, ch 1, d c back in same place as last d c on second motif. Ch 2, d c in same place, ch 3, s c in next s c, ch 3. In next ch-3 sp between 2 d c make d c, ch 2 and d c. Ch 1 and join this point to corresponding point of first motif as before, and complete as for 8th rnd of first motif.

Make 13 x 17 motifs, joining to adjacent motifs as second motif was joined to first, leaving 2 points free on each motif between joinings.

FILL-IN LACE . . . Starting at center ch 10, join. **1st rnd:** Ch 5, (tr in ring, ch 1) 15 times. Join to 4th ch of ch-5. **2nd rnd:** S c in next sp, ch 7, remove hook, insert it in center sp of any free point, and draw dropped loop through. * Ch 7, skip 1 sp on ring, s c in next sp, ch 7, remove hook, insert it in center sp of next free point and draw dropped loop through; repeat from * around, ending with ch-7, sl st in s c at base of 1st ch-7. Fasten off. Fill in all other sps in the same way.

Block to measure 60 x 80 inches.

HEART'S DESIRE

You've always wanted to fashion a flawlessly lovely cloth . . . one of inspired creation . . . truly luxurious! A lace cloth, not made casually, but a work of art . . . here it is . . . Heart's Desire, serene and dainty as a drift of plum blossoms!

HEART'S DESIRE

MATERIALS:

CLARK'S O.N.T. or J. & P. COATS BIG BALL BEST SIX CORD MERCERIZED CROCHET, size 30:

CLARK'S O.N.T.—36 balls of White or Ecru.

J. & P. COATS—36 balls of White or Ecru, or 48 balls of any color.

MILWARD'S Steel Crochet Hook No. 10.

GAUGE . . . Each motif measures 3¾ inches square before blocking. For a tablecloth about 72 x 90 inches, make 18 x 23 motifs.

FIRST MOTIF . . . Starting at center, ch 10, join with sl st to form a ring. **1st rnd:** Ch 4, 2 tr in ring, holding back on hook the last loop of each tr; thread over and draw through all 3 loops on hook (a cluster made). * Ch 4, make 3 tr in ring, holding back on hook the last loop of each tr; thread over and draw through all 4 loops on hook (another cluster). Repeat from * until 8 clusters in all are made; ch 4, sl st in tip of 1st cluster made. **2nd rnd:** Sl st in next ch, s c in sp, ch 4 (to count as tr), 2 tr in same sp as s c, * ch 4, 5 tr in next sp, ch 4, 3 tr in next sp. Repeat from * around, ending with ch 4, sl st in 4th st of ch-4 first made. **3rd rnd:** Ch 3 (to count as d c), d c in same place as sl st, * in next tr make d c, ch 2 and d c; 2 d c in next tr. Ch 4, s c in next 5 tr, ch 4, 2 d c in next tr. Repeat from * around, ending with ch 4, sl st in 3rd st of ch-3 first made.

4th rnd: Ch 3, d c in next 2 d c, * in next sp make d c, ch 2 and d c, d c in next 3 d c, (ch 4, s c in next s c) 5 times. Ch 4, d c in next 3 d c. Repeat from * around, joining as before. **5th rnd:** Ch 3, d c in next 2 d c, * ch 2, skip next d c, in next sp make 4 d c with ch-2 between. Ch 2, skip next d c, d c in next 3 d c. (Ch 4, skip next s c, s c in next loop) 4 times, ch 4, d c in next 3 d c. Repeat from * around; join. **6th rnd:** Ch 3, d c in next 2 d c, * (ch 2, d c in next sp) 3 times, ch 2, d c in same sp; (ch 2, d c in next sp) twice; ch 2, d c in next 3 d c. (Ch 4, skip next s c, s c in next loop) 3 times; ch 4, d c in next 3 d c. Repeat from * around; join.

7th rnd: Ch 3, d c in next 2 d c, * (ch 2, d c in next sp) 3 times, ch 2, 4 d c in next sp; (ch 2, d c in next sp) 3 times. Ch 2, d c in next 3 d c, (ch 4, skip next s c, s c in next loop) twice, ch 4, d c in next 3 d c. Repeat from * around; join. **8th rnd:** Ch 3, d c in next 2 d c, * (ch 2, d c in next sp) 3 times; ch 2, 4 d c in next sp, ch 3, 4 d c in next sp. (Ch 2, d c in next sp) 3 times, ch 2, d c in next 3 d c, ch 4, skip next s c, s c in next loop, ch 4, d c in next 3 d c. Repeat from * around; join. **9th rnd:** Ch 3, d c in next 2 d c, (ch 2, d c in next sp) 4 times. Ch 2, in next sp make 4 clusters (as in 1st rnd) with ch-2 between. (Ch 2, d c in next sp) 4 times, ch 2, d c in next 3 d c, skip

the next ch-4, the s c and the following ch-4, make d c in next 3 d c. Repeat from * around; join.

10th rnd: Sl st in next 2 d c, in following 2 ch and in next d c. Ch 3, * 2 d c in next sp, d c in next d c, ch 2, d c in next d c, 2 d c in next sp, d c in next d c, ch 2, d c in tip of next cluster, ch 2, skip next sp and cluster. In next sp make 5 tr with ch-2 between. Ch 2, skip next cluster and sp, d c in tip of next cluster. (Ch 2, d c in next d c, 2 d c in next sp, d c in next d c) twice; ch 4, skip next sp. D c in next 6 d c, holding back on hook the last loop of each d c; thread over and draw through all 7 loops on hook, ch 4, skip next sp, d c in next d c. Repeat from * around. Join and fasten off.

SECOND MOTIF . . . Work 1st 9 rnds as for first motif. **10th rnd:** Work as for 10th rnd of first motif, to the 3rd tr inclusive of first corner. Now (ch 1, s c in corresponding sp on first motif, ch 1, tr in same corner sp on motif in work) twice; ch 1, s c in corresponding sp on first motif, ch 1, skip next cluster and sp on motif in work, d c in tip of next cluster. (Ch 1, s c in corresponding sp on first motif, ch 1, d c in next d c on motif in work, 2 d c in next sp, d c in next d c) twice. Ch 2, s c in corresponding sp on first motif, ch 2, d c in next 6 d c on motif in work, holding back on hook the last loop of each d c; thread over and draw through all 7 loops on hook. This completes half of joining. Join other half to correspond and complete remainder of rnd as for first motif (no more joinings).

Make 18 x 23 motifs, joining them as second motif was joined to first (corner tr's are not joined).

EDGING . . . Attach thread to center tr at one corner of cloth, ch 8 (to count as d c and ch-5), d c in same place as thread was attached, * make sps, using ch 2 and d c over each of next 4 sps, sp over next bl, sp over sp, sp over bl. Ch 2, d c in next sp, ch 2, d c in tip of cluster, ch 2, d c in next sp. Ch 2, d c in next d c. (Sp over bl, sp over sp) twice; sp over next 3 sps, ch 2, d c in center tr at corner of next motif. Repeat from * around, making d c, ch 5 and d c at each corner. Join with sl st to 3rd st of ch-8 first made. **2nd rnd:** Sl st in sp, ch 4 (to count as tr) and complete a cluster in same sp. (Ch 5, make a cluster in same sp as last cluster) twice. * Ch 5, skip 1 sp, cluster in next sp. Repeat from * around, making 3 clusters with ch-5 between at each corner. Join last ch-5 to tip of 1st cluster made.

3rd rnd: Sl st in next sp, ch 5 (to count as d c and ch-2), d c in same sp, ch 2, d c in tip of next cluster, ch 5, d c in same place. * Ch 2, d c in next sp, ch 2, d c in same sp. Repeat from * around, working over each corner as for first corner; join. **4th rnd:** Sl st in sp, s c in same sp, * ch 5, skip 1 sp. In next sp make d c, ch 3 and d c; ch 5, skip 1 sp, s c in next sp. Repeat from * around, always having d c, ch 3 and d c in each corner sp. Join last ch-5 to 1st s c made. Fasten off.

Block cloth to measure 72 x 90 inches.

PINEAPPLE

Back from the rich Indies, Yankee clippers brought the lordly pineapple . . . and housewives borrowed its design to create the classic pineapple motif. See how charming it is, in repeating circles in this luncheon set with a flavor as traditional as the early New England that first used it.

MATERIALS: For best results use—

CLARK'S O.N.T. or J. & P. COATS BEST SIX CORD MERCERIZED CROCHET, size 50:

Small Ball:

CLARK'S O.N.T.—11 balls of White or Ecru, or 13 balls of any color,

OR

J. & P. COATS—8 balls of White or Ecru or 11 balls of any color.

Big Ball:

CLARK'S O.N.T. OR J. & P. COATS—5 balls of White or Ecru.

MILWARD'S Steel Crochet Hook No. 12.

Material is sufficient for a set consisting of centerpiece, 14 inches in diameter; 4 place doilies, 12 inches in diameter; 4 bread and butter plate doilies, 7 inches in diameter; and 4 glass doilies, 5½ inches in diameter.

CENTERPIECE . . . Starting at center, ch 16, join with sl st. **1st rnd:** Ch 3, 32 d c in ring, sl st in 3rd st of ch-3. **2nd rnd:** Ch 3, d c in each d c around; join to 3rd st of ch-3. **3rd rnd:** Ch 3, d c in same place as sl st, 2 d c in each d c around, sl st in 3rd st of ch-3. **4th rnd:** Repeat 2nd rnd. **5th rnd:** Ch 3, d c in same place as sl st, * ch 3, skip 2 d c, 2 d c in next d c. Repeat from * around, ending with ch 3, join to 3rd st of ch-3 (22 d c-groups). **6th rnd:** Sl st in next d c and in next sp, ch 3; in same sp make d c, ch 2 and 2 d c; in each ch-3 sp around make 2 d c, ch 2 and 2 d c; join. **7th rnd:** Sl st in next d c and in next ch-2 sp, ch 3, in same sp make d c, ch 2 and 2 d c; * ch 1, in next ch-2 sp make 2 d c, ch 2 and 2 d c (shell over shell). Repeat from * around, ending with ch-1; join.

8th to 12th rnds incl: Repeat 7th rnd, having an extra ch between each shell in each rnd. **13th rnd:** Sl st in next d c and in next sp, ch 3; in same sp make d c, ch 5 and 2 d c. * Ch 6, in next ch-2 sp make 2 d c, ch 2 and 2 d c, ch 6; in next ch-2 sp make 2 d c, ch 5 and 2 d c. Repeat from * around; join. **14th rnd:** Sl st in next d c and in next sp, ch 4, 12 tr in ch-5 of shell, * ch 5, in next ch-2 make 2 d c, ch 2 and 2 d c; ch 5, 13 tr in ch-5 of next shell. Repeat from * around, ending with ch 5, join.

15th rnd: Ch 5 (to count as tr and ch-1), tr in next tr; (ch 1, tr in next tr) 11 times; * ch 3, shell over next shell, ch 3, tr in next tr; (ch 1, tr in next tr) 12 times. Repeat from * around; join to 4th st of ch-5 first made. **16th rnd:** Sl st in 1st ch-1 sp, s c in same sp; * (ch 3, s c in next ch-1 sp) 11 times, ch 3, shell over next shell, ch 3, s c in next ch-1 sp. Repeat from * around, ending with ch 3, s c in 1st ch-3 loop. **17th rnd:** (Ch 3, s c in next loop) 10 times, * ch 3, shell over next shell; (ch 3, s c in next loop) 11 times. Repeat from * around, ending as in 16th rnd. **18th rnd:** (Ch 3, s c in next loop) 9 times, * ch 3, in ch-2 of next shell make 2 d c, ch 2, 2 d c, ch 2 and 2 d c. (Ch 3, s c in next loop) 10 times. Repeat from * around, ending as before.

19th rnd: (Ch 3, s c in next loop) 8 times, * ch 3, in next ch-2 make a shell, ch 2, shell in next ch-2. (Ch 3, s c in next loop) 9 times. Repeat from * around, ending as before. **20th rnd:** (Ch 3, s c in next loop) 7 times, * ch 3, shell over next shell, ch 1, shell in next ch-2 sp, ch 1, shell over next shell; (ch 3, s c in next loop) 8 times. Repeat from * around, ending as before. **21st rnd:** (Ch 3, s c in next loop) 6 times; * (ch 3, shell over next shell) 3 times; (ch 3, s c in next loop) 7 times. Repeat from * around, ending as before. **22nd rnd:** (Ch 3, s c in next loop) 5 times, * ch 3; shell over next shell; (ch 4, shell over next shell) twice; (ch 3, s c in next loop) 6 times. Repeat from * around.

23rd rnd: (Ch 3, s c in next loop) 4 times; * ch 3, shell over next shell, ch 5; in next shell make 2 d c, ch 5 and 2 d c; ch 5, shell over next shell; (ch 3, s c in next loop) 5 times. Repeat from * around. **24th rnd:** (Ch 3, s c in next loop) 3 times; * ch 3, shell over next shell, ch 3, 14 tr in next shell, ch 3, shell over next shell; (ch 3, s c in next loop) 4 times. Repeat from * around. **25th rnd:** (Ch 3, s c in next loop) twice; * ch 3, shell over next shell, ch 3, tr in next tr; (ch 1, tr in next tr) 13 times; ch 3, shell over next shell; (ch 3, s c in next loop) 3 times. Repeat from * around.

26th rnd: Ch 3, s c in next loop, * ch 3, shell over next shell; (ch 3, s c in next ch-1 sp) 13 times; ch 3, shell over next shell; (ch 3, s c in next loop) twice.

Repeat from * around. **27th rnd:** * Ch 4, shell over next shell; (ch 3, s c in next loop) 12 times; ch 3, shell over next shell; ch 4, s c in next loop. Repeat from * around, ending with ch 4, sl st in 1st s c. Fasten off. **28th row:** Attach thread to ch-2 of next shell of previous rnd, ch 3; make d c, ch 2 and 2 d c in same shell; (ch 3, s c in next loop) 11 times; ch 3, shell over next shell. Ch 3, turn.

29th row: Shell over shell; (ch 3, s c in next loop) 10 times; ch 3, shell over next shell; ch 3, turn. Continue in this manner, having 1 ch-3 loop less on each row until 36th row is completed. **37th row:** Shell over shell; (ch 3, s c in next loop) twice; ch 3, shell over shell—*1 loop remaining at point.* Ch 3, turn. Make shell over shell, ch 4, s c in next loop, ch 4, 2 d c in next shell, ch 1, sl st back in ch-2 of last shell; ch 1,

(Continued on next page)

PINEAPPLE

(continued from preceding page)

2 d c where last 2 d c were made. Fasten off. Attach thread to ch-2 of next shell of 27th rnd and complete the next point in same manner. Continue until all 11 points have been worked; then work as follows:

1st rnd: Attach thread to tip of one point where shells were joined, ch 3, in same place where ch-3 was joined make d c, ch 2 and 2 d c. * (Ch 3, shell in next turning ch, between 2 rows) 5 times; ch 2, d c in ch-2 of shell preceding ch-4 (on 27th rnd), holding back the last loop of this d c and next d c on hook; d c in ch-2 of next shell (where thread was attached, to work point); thread over and draw through all loops on hook; (ch 3, shell in turning ch between 2 rows) 5 times; ch 3, shell at tip of next point, where shells were joined. Repeat from * around. Join last ch-3 to 3rd st of ch-3. **2nd rnd:** Sl st in next d c and in next sp, ch 8, s c in 5th ch from hook (a p made). D c in same place as sl st, * ch 3, s c under next ch-3, ch 3; in next shell make d c, p and d c. Repeat from * 4 more times, ch 3, s c in next d c, ch 3; in next shell make d c, p and d c. Ch 3, s c under next ch-3. Continue thus around. Fasten off.

PLACE DOILIES (Make 4) . . . Starting at center ch 12. Join with sl st. **1st rnd:** Ch 3 (to count as d c), 26 d c in ring. Join with sl st in 3rd st of ch-3. **2nd rnd:** Ch 3, d c in same st as sl st, 2 d c in each st around (54 d c). Join. **3rd to 9th rnds incl:** Same as 5th to 11th rnds incl. of centerpiece—18 d c-groups on 3rd rnd. **10th rnd:** Same as 13th rnd of centerpiece, making ch-5 (instead of ch-6) between shells. **11th rnd:** Same as 14th rnd of centerpiece, making ch-4 (instead of ch-5) between shells and tr-groups (9 tr-groups in rnd). Starting with 15th rnd of centerpiece, work as for centerpiece until place doily is completed.

BREAD and BUTTER PLATE DOILIES (Make 4) . . . Ch 16, join with sl st. **1st rnd:** Ch 3 (to count as d c), 41 d c in ring. **2nd to 5th rnds incl:** Same as 5th to 8th rnds of centerpiece—*14 d c-groups on 2nd rnd.* **6th rnd:** Sl st in next d c and in next sp, ch 3, in same sp make d c, ch 5, 2 d c; * ch 4, shell over next shell, ch 4, in sp of next shell make 2 d c, ch 5 and 2 d c. Repeat from * around. Join. **7th rnd:** Sl st in next d c and in next sp, ch 4 (to count as tr), 10 tr in ch-5 sp, * ch 3, shell over shell, ch 3, 11 tr in next ch-5 sp. Repeat from * around, ending with ch 3, join (7 tr groups in rnd). **8th rnd:** Ch 5 *(to count as tr and ch-1),* tr in next tr; (ch 1, tr in next tr) 9 times; * ch 3, shell over next shell, ch 3, tr in next tr; (ch 1, tr in next tr) 10 times. Repeat from * around; join to 4th st of ch-5 first made.

9th rnd: Same as 16th rnd of centerpiece making (ch-3, s c in next ch-1 sp) 9 times—instead of 11 times. **10th rnd:** (Ch 3, s c in next loop) 8 times, * ch 3, shell over next shell; (ch 3, s c in next loop)

9 times. Repeat from * around, ending with sl st in s c at base of 1st loop made. Fasten off. Work is now done in rows. **11th row:** Attach thread to ch-2 of next shell of previous rnd, ch 3; make d c, ch 2 and 2 d c in same shell; (ch 3, s c in next loop) 8 times; ch 3, shell over next shell. Ch 3, turn. **12th row:** Shell over shell; (ch 3, s c in next loop) 7 times; ch 3, shell over next shell; ch 3, turn. Continue in this manner, having 1 ch-3 loop less on each row until 16th row is completed. **17th row:** Same as 37th row of centerpiece. Fasten off. Attach thread to ch-2 of next shell on 10th rnd and complete the next point in same manner. Continue thus until all 7 points have been worked. Then work as follows:

1st rnd: Attach thread to tip of any point where shells were joined, ch 3; in same place where thread was attached make d c, ch 2 and 2 d c. * (Ch 3, shell in next turning ch) 3 times, ch 2, d c in next turning ch, skip next shell, d c under starting ch of next shell, (ch 3, shell in next turning ch) 3 times, ch 3, shell in tip of point, where shells meet. Repeat from * around. Join. **2nd rnd:** Sl st in next d c and in next sp, ch 8 (to count as d c and ch-5 for a picot), s c in 5th ch from hook—*a p made.* D c in same place as sl st, * ch 3, s c under next ch-3, ch 3; in next shell make d c, p and d c. Repeat from * 2 more times, ch 3, s c between next 2 d c's, ch 3; in next shell make d c, p and d c. Ch 3, s c under next ch-3. Continue thus around. Join and fasten off.

GLASS DOILIES (Make 4) . . . Starting at center, ch 8. Join. **1st rnd:** Ch 3, 19 d c in ring. Join. **2nd rnd:** Ch 3, d c in same place as sl st, * ch 2, skip 1 d c, 2 d c in next d c. Repeat from * around, ending with ch 2, sl st in 3rd st of ch-3 first made (10 d c-groups). **3rd rnd:** Sl st in next d c and in next sp, ch 3. In same sp make d c, ch 2 and 2 d c, * ch 3, shell in next sp. Repeat from * around, ending with ch 3, sl st in top st of ch-3 first made. **4th rnd:** Ch 3; in same sp make d c, ch 5 and 2 d c, * ch 4, shell in sp of next shell, ch 4. In sp of next shell make 2 d c, ch 5 and 2 d c. Repeat from * around, ending with ch 4, sl st in top st of ch-3 first made. **5th rnd:** Same as 7th rnd of bread and butter plate doily (5 tr-groups in rnd). Work remainder of this doily as for bread and butter plate doily.

Block all pieces to measurements given.

MODERN RUSTIC

Give a gay air of informality to your luncheon table with this heavy textured two-toned luncheon set (grand with peasant pottery), modern as tomorrow, but with a cute checked air most beguiling in its crispness.

MATERIALS:

J. & P. COATS KNIT-CRO-SHEEN, 4 balls of White or Ecru for main color (to be referred to as "M"), and 8 balls of a contrasting color (to be referred to as "C").

MILWARD'S Steel Crochet Hook No. 8 or 9.

The above amount of materials is sufficient for 4 place mats, each about 11½ x 17 inches, and a center mat about 14 x 32 inches.

GAUGE . . . 12 d c make 1 inch; 4 rows make 1 inch.

PLACE MATS—(Make 4) . . . Starting at long side, with C color ch 192 (to measure about 18 inches). **1st row:** D c in 4th ch from hook, d c in each ch across (190 d c, counting turning ch-3 as 1 d c). Ch 3, turn. **2nd row:** D c in each d c across. Ch 3, turn. **3rd row:** D c in each of 5 d c; d c in next d c, leaving the last 2 loops on hook, drop C, attach M color, and * draw through 2 loops. Then, holding C along top of previous row, make d c in each of next 4 d c (thus concealing C); d c in next d c, leaving the last 2 loops on hook, drop M, pick up C and draw through 2 loops; d c in next d c, leaving the last

2 loops on hook, drop C, pick up M and draw through 2 loops; d c in each of next 5 d c, leaving the last 2 loops on hook and concealing C as before; drop M, pick up C and draw through 2 loops. Then, holding M along top of previous row, make d c in each of 4 d c, leaving the last 2 loops on hook (thus concealing M); drop C, pick up M. Repeat from * across, ending row with 5 M d c and 7 C d c. Ch 3, turn. Hereafter work as follows, changing color and concealing unused color as before: **4th row:** 6 C d c, * 3 M d c, 5 C d c, 3 M d c, 4 C d c. Repeat from * across, ending with 7 C d c. Ch 3, turn. **5th row:** 6 C d c, * 5 M d c, 1 C d c, 5 M d c, 4 C d c. Repeat from * across, ending row with 7 C d c. Ch 3, turn. **6th row:** 17 C d c, * 4 M d c, 11 C d c. Repeat from * across, ending row with 18 C d c. Ch. 3, turn. The last 4 rows (3rd to 6th rows incl.) constitute the pattern. Repeat pattern 10 more times, but omit the 6th row of the last pattern. Break off M, and work 2 rows of C d c. Break off.

CENTER MAT . . . Starting at short side with C, ch 161 (to measure about 14 inches). Work exactly as for place mats until piece measures 31½ inches. Break off M, and work 2 rows of C d c. Break off.

LUCKY STAR

It's been our Lucky Star . . . this precious design
that's made crochet history! Lots of twinkle in its
stellar pattern . . . in the star-like tendrils, too.

MATERIALS:

CLARK'S BIG BALL MERCERIZED CROCHET,
size 20, 44 balls of White or Ecru.

MILWARD'S Steel Crochet Hook No. 11 or 12.

GAUGE . . . Each motif measures about 4½ inches in
diameter. When completed, tablecloth measures about
72 x 90 inches.

MOTIF . . . Starting at center, ch 8, join with sl st
to form a ring. **1st rnd:** Ch 5, * d c in ring, ch 2. Repeat from * 6 more times. Join last ch-2 with sl st to
3rd st of ch-5 first made (8 sps). **2nd rnd:** Sl st in
ch-2 sp, ch 3, 2 d c in same sp, ch 2, * 3 d c in next
sp, ch 2. Repeat from * around. Join last ch-2 with
sl st to 3rd st of ch-3 first made. **3rd rnd:** Ch 3, d c
in same place as sl st, * d c in next d c, 2 d c in next
d c, ch 2, 2 d c in next d c. Repeat from * around,
ending with ch 2. Join to 3rd st of ch-3 first made.
4th rnd: Ch 3, d c in same place as sl st, * d c in each
of next 3 d c, 2 d c in next d c, ch 2, 2 d c in next d c.
Repeat from * around, ending with ch 2. Join. **5th**

rnd: Ch 3, d c in same place as sl st, * d c in each of next 5 d c, 2 d c in next d c, ch 3, 2 d c in next d c. Repeat from * around, ending with ch 3. Join. **6th rnd:** Sl st in next d c, ch 3, * d c in each of next 6 d c, ch 3, s c in ch-3 sp, ch 3, skip 1 d c, d c in next d c. Repeat from * around, ending with ch 3. Join. **7th rnd:** Sl st in next d c, ch 3, * d c in each of next 4 d c, ch 4, s c in ch-3 sp, s c in next s c, s c in next ch-3 sp, ch 4, skip 1 d c, d c in next d c. Repeat from * around. Join. **8th rnd:** Sl st in next d c, ch 3, * d c in each of next 2 d c, ch 5, s c in ch-4 sp, s c in each of next 3 s c, s c in next sp, ch 5, skip 1 d c, d c in next d c. Repeat from * around, ending with ch 5. Join. **9th rnd:** Sl st in next d c, ch 3, 2 d c in same place as sl st, holding back the last loop of each d c on hook; thread over and draw through all loops on hook, ch 1 to fasten (thus a 3-d c cluster is made—counting ch-3 as 1 d c); * ch 6, s c in ch-5 loop, s c in each of next 5 s c, s c in next loop, ch 6, skip 1 d c, 3-d c cluster in next d c. Repeat from * around, ending with ch 6, sl st in tip of 1st cluster made. **10th rnd:** S c in same place as sl st, ** ch 5, skip 3 s c, tr in next s c, * ch 2, tr in same s c. Repeat from * 2 more times, ch 5, s c in tip of next cluster. Repeat from ** around, ending with ch 5. Join. **11th rnd:** Ch 6, d c in same place as sl st, * ch 3, 4 s c in ch-5 loop, s c in ch-2 sp, ch 3; in next ch-2 sp make d c, ch 3, d c; ch 3, s c in next ch-2

sp, 4 s c in next ch-5 loop, ch 3; in next s c make d c, ch 3, d c. Repeat from * around, ending with ch 3. Join with sl st to 3rd st of ch-6 first made. **12th rnd:** Sl st in ch-3 sp, ch 6, d c in same sp, * ch 3, s c in next ch-3 sp, ch 2, skip 2 s c, s c in next s c, ch 2, s c in next sp, ch 3; in next ch-3 sp (between d c's) make d c, ch 3, d c. Repeat from * around, ending with ch 3, sl st in 3rd st of ch-6 first made. Fasten and break off. This completes one motif.

Make 16 x 20 motifs, and sew together on wrong side with neat over-and-over stitches, joining 2 points of each motif to 2 points of adjacent motifs, leaving 2 points free on each motif, between joinings, to be filled in later.

FILL-IN LACE . . . Ch 8, join with sl st to form ring. **1st rnd:** Ch 5, * d c in ring, ch 2. Repeat from * 6 more times. Join with sl st to 3rd st of ch-5 first made (8 sps). **2nd rnd:** S c in same place as sl st, * ch 18, s c at joining of 2 motifs, ch 18, s c in same place as 1st s c was made, s c in next sp, ch 9, s c in next point on motif, ch 9, s c in same sp on ring where last s c was made, s c in next sp, ch 9, s c in next point, ch 9, s c in same sp on ring where last s c was made, s c in next d c. Repeat from * around. Join with sl st. Fasten and break off.

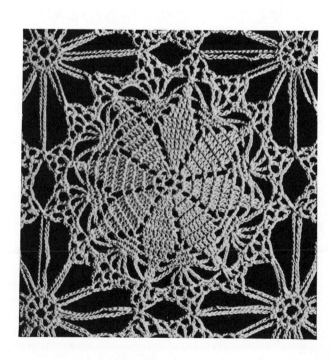

KATE GREENAWAY

With its scatterings of dainty little blossoms and its prim center wreath, it has a quaint Kate Greenaway air. Daintily white, and as fresh as a snowdrop, with the adorable round doilies that make such a charming luncheon service.

MATERIALS: For best results use—

CLARK'S O.N.T. or J. & P. COATS BEST SIX CORD MERCERIZED CROCHET, size 30:

Small Ball:

CLARK'S O.N.T.—14 balls of White or Ecru, or 21 balls of any color.

OR

J. & P. COATS—11 balls of White or Ecru or 14 balls of any color.

Big Ball:

CLARK'S O.N.T.—5 balls of White or Ecru.

OR

J. & P. COATS—5 balls of White or Ecru, or 7 balls of any color.

MILWARD'S Steel Crochet Hook No. 10 or 11.

This amount is sufficient for a set consisting of a centerpiece about 16 inches in diameter; 4 place doilies about 12½ inches in diameter; 4 bread and butter plate doilies about 7½ inches in diameter; and 4 glass doilies about 5 inches in diameter.

GAUGE . . . 4 sps or bls make 1 inch; 4 rows make 1 inch.

CENTERPIECE . . . Starting at bottom of chart, ch 68 (16 ch sts to 1 inch). **1st row:** Tr in 11th ch from hook, * ch 3, skip 3 ch, tr in next ch (2 sps made). Repeat from * across (15 sps made). Ch 18, turn. **2nd row:** Tr in 11th ch from hook, ch 3, skip 3 ch, tr in next ch, ch 3, tr in last tr made on previous row (thus increasing 3 sps at beginning of row). Ch 3, tr in next tr (thus making sp over sp). Make sp over next 14 sps, ch 7, tr in same ch as last tr made. * Ch 7, turn; tr in 4th st of previous ch-7. Repeat from * once more, turn, sl st to 4th st of last ch-7 (3 end sps increased). Ch 18, turn.

3rd row: Inc. 3 sps as before, work sp over 21 sps, inc. 3 sps at end of row. Ch 14, turn. **4th row:** Inc. 2 sps along ch-14, make sp over next 13 sps, 3 tr in next sp, tr in next tr (bl made over sp). Make sp over next 13 sps; ch 7, tr in same ch as last tr, ch 7, turn; tr in 4th st of last ch-7 made (2 sps increased). Ch 14, turn. **5th row:** Inc. 2 sps, sp over 14 sps, bl over next sp, tr in next 3 tr, tr in next tr (thus making bl over bl). Make bl over next sp, make 14 sps, inc. 2 sps. Ch 10, turn.

6th row: Tr in last tr made (1 sp increased); work across previous row, following chart. Ch 7, tr in same ch as last tr, turn, sl st to 4th st of ch-7 (1 sp increased). Ch 10, turn. Now follow chart until 39 rows are made (when there are no increases, ch 7 to turn). **40th row:** Sl st across 1st sp and in next tr, ch 7 (this counts as tr and ch-3). Follow chart across to within last sp of previous row (1 sp decreased at each end). Now follow chart to top. Do not break off, but work s c all around, keeping work flat. Break off.

PLACE DOILIES . . . Ch 60 and follow chart (13 sps on 1st row). Work s c all around doily.

BREAD and BUTTER PLATE DOILIES . . . Ch 36 and follow chart (7 sps on 1st row). Work s c all around doily.

GLASS DOILIES . . . Ch 28 and follow chart (5 sps on 1st row). Work s c all around doily.

Block all pieces to measurements.

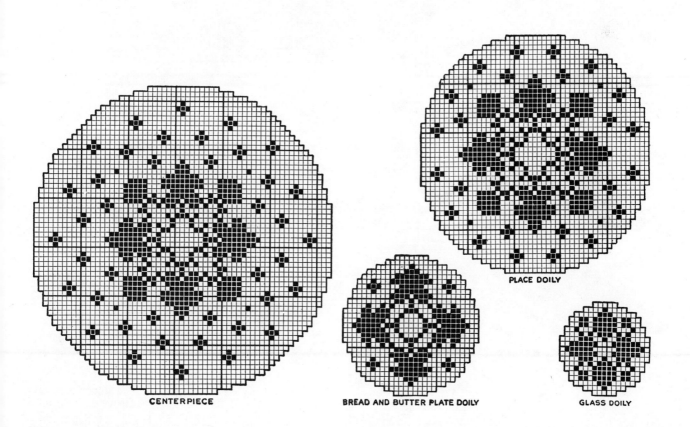

CENTERPIECE

BREAD AND BUTTER PLATE DOILY

PLACE DOILY

GLASS DOILY

FANCY FREE

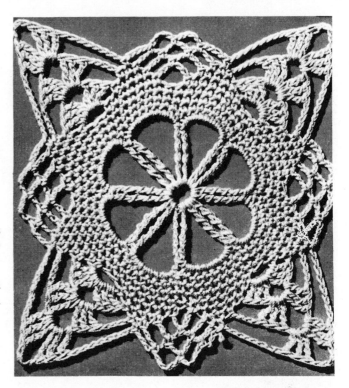

MATERIALS:

CLARK'S O.N.T. or **J. & P. COATS BIG BALL BEST SIX CORD MERCERIZED CROCHET,** size 20, 32 balls of White or Ecru.

MILWARD'S Steel Crochet Hook No. 8 or 9.

GAUGE . . . Each motif measures about 3¼ inches square before blocking. For a tablecloth 60 x 80 inches (including edging), make 16 x 22 motifs.

FIRST MOTIF . . . Starting at center, ch 9, join with sl st. **1st rnd:** Ch 6, tr tr in ring. (Ch 7, 2 tr tr in ring) 7 times, ch 7, sl st in 6th ch of ch-6—*8 sps made.* **2nd rnd:** In each ch-7 sp make 9 s c; join. **3rd rnd:** * S c in next 8 s c, skip 1 s c. Repeat from * around; join. **4th and 5th rnds:** S c in each s c around. **6th rnd:** Sl st in next s c, * s c in next 7 s c, ch 5, skip 1 s c. Repeat from * around, ending with ch 5, sl st in 1st s c made. **7th rnd:** Sl st in next s c, * s c in next 5 s c; in next ch-5 loop make 3 d c, ch 4 and 3 d c. Skip 1 s c, s c in next 5 s c, ch 4. S c in ch-5 loop, ch 4, skip 1 s c. Repeat from * around, ending with ch 4, sl st in 1st s c.

8th rnd: * S c in next 3 s c, ch 4, in ch-4 loop between d c-groups make 3 d c, ch 4 and 3 d c. Ch 4, skip 1 s c, s c in next 3 s c. (Ch 4, s c in next loop) twice; ch 4, skip 1 s c. Repeat from * around, ending with ch 4, sl st in 1st s c made. **9th rnd:** * S c in next s c, ch 8; in ch-4 loop between d c-groups make 3 d c, ch 4 and 3 d c. Ch 8, skip 1 s c, s c in next s c. (Ch 4, s c in next loop) 3 times; ch 4, skip 1 s c. Repeat from * around, ending with ch 4, sl st in 1st s c. Fasten off.

SECOND MOTIF . . . Work 1st 8 rnds as for first motif. **9th rnd:** S c in next s c, ch 8, 3 d c in ch-4 between d c-groups, ch 2, sl st in corresponding loop of first motif, ch 2, 3 d c back in same place as last 3 d c on second motif. Ch 4, sl st in next loop on first motif, ch 4, skip 1 s c of second motif, s c in next s c, ch 4, s c in next loop, * ch 2, sl st in corresponding loop on first motif, ch 2, s c back in next loop on second motif. Repeat from * once more, ch 4, skip 1 s c, s c in next s c on second motif, join next ch-8 and the following ch-4 loops at corner as previous loops were joined. Complete as for 9th rnd of first motif. Fasten off.

Make 16 x 22 motifs, joining as second motif was joined to first (where 4 corners meet, join 3rd and 4th corners to joining of other corners).

EDGING . . . 1st rnd: Attach thread to 3rd d c of second 3-d c group at corner, s c in same d c. * Ch 5, s c in next ch-8 loop, (ch 5, s c in next loop) 4 times. Ch 5, s c in next ch-8 loop, ch 5, s c in next d c, ch 5, s c in joining, ch 5, skip 2 d c, s c in next d c. Repeat from * around, making s c, ch 5 and s c at each corner, and ending with ch 2, d c in 1st s c made. **2nd to 7th rnds incl:** S c in loop just made, * ch 5, s c in next loop. Repeat from * around, making s c, ch 5 and s c at corners, and ending with ch 2, d c in 1st s c made.

8th rnd: Ch 6, tr tr in loop just made, * ch 3, 2 tr tr in next loop. Repeat from * around, making 2 tr tr, ch 3 and 2 tr tr in each corner loop, and ending with ch 3, sl st in 6th ch of ch-6. **9th rnd:** Sl st in next tr tr, * 3 s c in next ch-3 loop, ch 4. Repeat from * around. Join and fasten off.

Block cloth to measure 60 x 80 inches.

ARABIAN NIGHTS

Frankly fabulous, this dramatic cloth . . . with
the look of Oriental splendor in its motifs . . .
gracefully webbed with spoke-like joinings.

MATERIALS:
CLARK'S O.N.T. "BRITA-SHEEN," 15 balls.
MILWARD'S Steel Crochet Hook No. 7.

GAUGE . . . Each motif measures 5 inches across center, from picot to picot, before blocking. For a tablecloth about 60 x 80 inches, make 11 x 15 motifs.

FIRST MOTIF . . . Starting at center, ch 2. **1st rnd:** 6 s c in 2nd ch from hook. Do not join rnds. **2nd rnd:** 2 s c in each s c around. **3rd rnd:** * S c in next s c, 2 s c in next s c. Repeat from * around. **4th to 8th rnds incl:** S c in each s c around, increasing 6 s c in each rnd, having increases directly over previous increases (48 s c on 8th rnd). Sl st in next s c. **9th rnd:** * Ch 5, skip 1 s c, s c in next s c. Repeat from * around, ending with ch 2, d c in sl st.

10th and 11th rnds: * Ch 5, s c in next loop. Repeat from * around, ending with ch 2, d c in d c of previous rnd. **12th and 13th rnds:** Same as 11th rnd, making ch-6 loops (instead of ch-5) and ending with ch 3, d c in d c. **14th rnd:** * Ch 5, s c in next loop, ch 8, s c in next loop. Repeat from * around, ending with ch 7, s c in d c. **15th rnd:** * 5 s c in next loop. In next loop make 2 s c, ch 3, s c in 3rd ch from hook *(picot made)*, 2 s c, p, 2 s c, p, 2 s c. Repeat from * around, ending with sl st in 1st s c. Fasten off. This completes one motif.

SECOND MOTIF . . . Work as for first motif to within 2nd p on 15th rnd. Ch 1, s c in a corresponding p on first motif, ch 1, complete p on second motif, and continue rnd as for first motif, joining 2nd p of next ch-8 loop to corresponding p on first motif.

Make 11 x 15 motifs, joining all motifs as second was joined to first, leaving four ch-8 loops free on each side of joining.

FILL-IN LACE . . . Starting at center, ch 2. **1st rnd:** 6 s c in 2nd ch from hook. Do not join rnds. **2nd rnd:** 2 s c in each s c around (12 s c in rnd). Sl st in next s c. **3rd rnd:** Ch 8, sl st in center p of free loop of one motif, * s c in each ch across, s c in next s c of center, ch 11, sl st in free p on next loop of same motif (preceding joining), s c in each ch across, s c in next s c of center, ch 11, sl st in next free p on next loop of next motif (following joining). S c in each ch across, s c in next s c of center, ch 8, sl st in center p of next free loop of same motif. Repeat from * around. Join and fasten off. Fill in all sps between joinings in same way.

Block cloth to measure 60 x 80 inches.

Welcome color to your table, fresh, lovely color, using self-shading threads in four pastel shades to create an effect as enchanting as a spring bouquet! Such a refreshing change from all white, but do keep your china and centerpiece simple to give your lace cloth star role!

MAYDAY BOUQUET

MAYDAY BOUQUET

MATERIALS: For best results use—

CLARK'S O.N.T. or J. & P. COATS BEST SIX CORD MERCERIZED CROCHET, size 30:

Small Ball:

CLARK'S O.N.T.—51 balls of one self-shading color; 48 balls of second self-shading color; and 45 balls each of a third and fourth self-shading color.

OR

J. & P. COATS—34 balls of one self-shading color; 32 balls of second self-shading color; and 30 balls each of a third and fourth self-shading color.

Big Ball:

J. & P. COATS—17 balls of one self-shading color; 16 balls of second self-shading color; and 15 balls each of a third and fourth self-shading color.

MILWARD'S Steel Crochet Hook No. 10.

GAUGE . . . Each motif measures 3 inches from point to opposite point across center, and 2⅝ inches from side to side, before blocking. For a table-cloth about 60 x 80 inches, make 737 motifs.

FIRST MOTIF OF FIRST STRIP . . . Starting at center, with first color, ch 10, join with sl st. **1st rnd:** Ch 3, 2 d c in ring; (ch 1, 3 d c in ring) 5 times, ch 1, sl st in 3rd ch of ch-3. Now pick up the back loop of each d c throughout. **2nd rnd:** Ch 3, d c in same place as sl st, * d c in next d c, 2 d c in next d c, ch 2, 2 d c in next d c. Repeat from * around. Join last ch-2 with sl st to 3rd st of ch-3. **3rd rnd:** Ch 3, d c in same place as sl st, * d c in next 3 d c, 2 d c in next d c, ch 3, 2 d c in next d c. Repeat from * around; join.

4th rnd: Sl st in next 3 d c, ch 8 (to count as tr and ch-4), skip 2 d c, s c in last d c of this d c-group, * ch 4, s c in 1st d c of next d c-group, ch 4, skip 2 d c, tr in next d c. Ch 4, skip 2 d c, s c in last d c of same group. Repeat from * around. Join last ch-4 to 4th ch of ch-8. **5th rnd:** * Ch 4, 2 tr in same place as sl st, holding back the last loop of each tr on hook; thread over and draw through all loops on hook, ch 1 to fasten (a cluster made). Ch 4, sl st in ch-1 of cluster (a p made). Ch 4, sl st at base of cluster, ch 4, cluster in same place as last sl st, ch-4 p, ch 2, skip next ch-4. In next ch-4 loop make tr, ch 1 and tr. Ch 2, 2 tr in next tr, holding back on hook the last loop of each tr,

and complete a cluster. Ch-4 p, ch 4, sl st at base of cluster. Repeat from * around, ending with cluster in place where first 2 clusters were made, p, ch-4, sl st at base of cluster. Fasten off.

SECOND MOTIF . . . With second color, work as for first motif until the first cluster of 5th rnd is completed. Then work as follows: Ch 1, sl st in p of corresponding cluster on first motif, ch 1, sl st back in ch-1 of cluster on 2nd motif, ch 4, sl st at base of same cluster, ch 4, cluster in same place as last cluster. Now make a p, joining it to corresponding p on first motif as first 2 p's were joined. Continue as for 5th rnd of first motif, joining next 2 p's of motif in work to the 2 adjacent p's of first motif as before and complete rnd (no more joinings). Join and fasten off. Make 27 more motifs, alternating first and second colors, joining to previous one as second was joined to first, having five clusters free at each side between joinings.

Join second strip of motifs to left of first strip, beginning from top of chart as follows:

FIRST MOTIF OF SECOND STRIP . . . With third color, work as for second motif of first strip, joining 4 p's as before to 4 p's of first motif of first strip, leaving a cluster, a 2-tr group and a cluster free between joinings.

SECOND MOTIF OF SECOND STRIP . . . With fourth color, work as for second motif of first strip until first cluster on 5th rnd is completed. Ch 1, s c in 3rd free p of second motif of first strip, counting from joining. Continue as for 5th rnd of second motif of first strip until 2 more p's are joined. Join the next p to joining where p's of first strip were joined. Continue as before until 2 more p's are joined. Join next p to next joining. Then join the next 3 p's as before and complete rnd. Fasten off. Follow chart from right to left for joining of motifs; detail in upper right-hand corner shows sequence of colors.

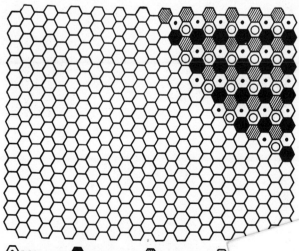

⊙ **FIRST COLOR** ⬡ **SECOND COLOR** ◩ **THIRD COLOR** ◎

FAMILY CIRCLE

MATERIALS: CLARK'S O.N.T. or J. & P. COATS BIG BALL BEST SIX CORD MERCERIZED CROCHET, *size 20, 31 balls of White or Ecru.*

MILWARD'S *steel crochet hook No. 7.*

GAUGE: 5 sps make 1 inch; 5 rows make 1·inch.

Completed tablecloth measures about 83 inches in diameter.

A never-ending circle of filet beauty—a round cloth
that enmeshes a charming design in its center
and a border that ripples symmetry and grace.

There are 10 spaces
between heavy lines

BOTTOM

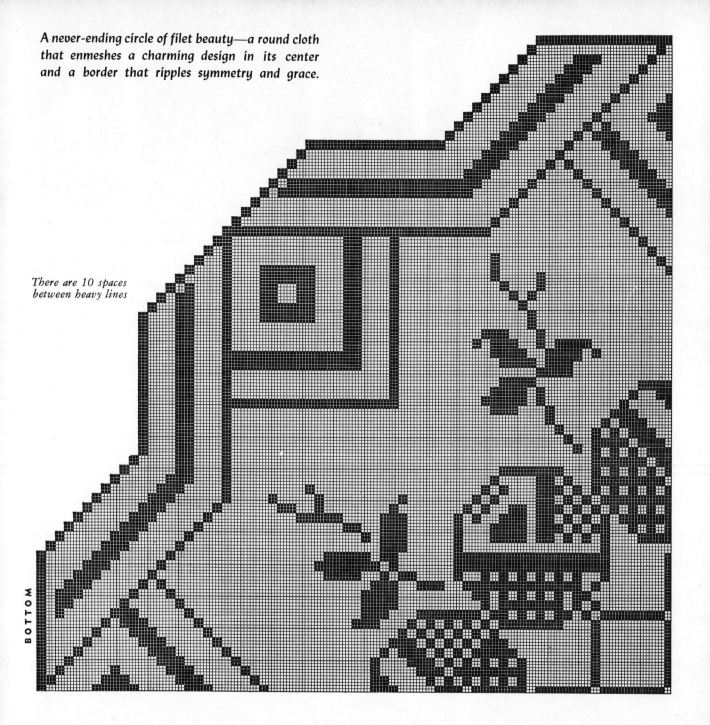

Starting at "BOTTOM" on chart, ch 267 (15 ch sts to 1 inch). **1st row:** D c in 4th ch from hook and in each ch across (265 d c, counting turning ch as 1 d c). Ch 3, turn. **2nd and 3rd rows:** Skip 1st d c, d c in each d c across, d c in 3rd st of turning ch. Ch 3 to turn at end of 2nd row and ch 11 to turn at end of 3rd row. **4th row:** D c in 4th ch from hook, d c in next 7 ch, d c in next d c (3 bls increased); ch 2, skip 2 d c, d c in next d c (1 sp); make 38 more sps, d c in next 9 d c (3 bls); 4 sps, 3 bls, 38 sps, ch 2, make a foundation d c in 3rd st of turning ch—*to make a foundation d c, thread over, insert hook in ch and draw loop through, thread over and draw through 1 loop, thus making a ch st; thread over and finish as for a d c—* * make another foundation d c by inserting

hook in ch-1 of previous foundation d c. Repeat from * until 8 foundation d c are made; then make a d c in the usual way (3 bls increased). Ch 3, turn. **5th and 6th rows:** Bl over bl, and sp over sp. Ch 11 to turn at end of 6th row. **7th row:** D c in 4th ch from hook, d c in next 7 d c, d c in next d c; 15 sps, d c in next 2 ch, d c in next d c (1 bl); make 8 more bls, 15 sps, 3 bls, 10 sps, 3 bls, 15 sps, 9 bls, 15 sps; inc. 3 bls as before. Ch 3, turn. Starting at 8th row, follow chart to top. Chart shows ¼ of design. To make second half of each row, repeat first half, starting from center and working back. When work reaches top row, reverse the design by working back to the first row.

For napkins, we suggest No. 2 on page 113.

DINNER AT EIGHT

DINNER AT EIGHT

MATERIALS: CLARK'S O.N.T. or J. & P. COATS BIG BALL BEST SIX CORD MERCERIZED CROCHET, *size 30, 14 balls of White or Ecru, or 19 balls of any color.*

MILWARD'S *steel crochet hook No. 10 or 11.*

3¾ yds. of linen, 72 inches wide.

These materials are sufficient for a tablecloth 71 x 90 inches, and 8 napkins, each about 18 inches square.

GAUGE: 6 sps make 1 inch; 6 rows make 1 inch.

CORNERS (Make 4)... Starting at bottom of chart A, ch 417 (18 ch sts to 1 inch). **1st row:** D c in 4th ch from hook, d c in each ch across (415 d c, counting turning ch as 1 d c). Ch 3, turn. **2nd to 5th rows incl:** Skip 1st d c, d c in next 3 d c (1 bl); * ch 2, skip 2 d c, d c in next d c. Repeat from * across, ending with d c in last 3 d c, d c in 3rd st of turning ch. Ch 3, turn. **6th row:** 1 bl, 21 sps, d c in next 2 ch, d c in next d c (1 bl); make 3 more bls; follow chart across. Ch 3, turn. Starting at 7th row, follow chart until 60 rows are made. Fasten off. **61st row:** Attach thread to 4th d c of 79th bl, counting back from end of previous row. Ch 3, d c in next 3 d c, 8 sps, 4 bls, 10 sps, 1 bl, 12 sps, 3 bls, 1 sp, 2 bls, 2 sps, 3 bls, 3 sps, 3 bls, 5 sps, 1 bl. Ch 3, turn. Follow chart to top; fasten off.

INSERTION... Starting at bottom of chart B, ch 74. **1st row:** D c in 4th ch from hook, d c in next 2

ch, ch 2, skip 2 ch, d c in next 4 ch. (Ch 2, skip 2 ch, d c in next ch) 4 times; d c in next 3 ch, ch 2, skip 2 ch, d c in next 4 ch; 4 sps, 1 bl, 3 sps, 2 bls, 3 sps, 1 bl. Follow chart B until 114 rows are completed. Fasten off. Attach thread at A on chart, ch 3 and follow chart to end. Reverse chart and work back to 1st row, making corner as before. This completes one half of insertion. Work other half to correspond. Fasten off. Sew both short ends together.

NAPKINS (Make 8)... Starting at bottom of chart C, ch 75. **1st row:** D c in 4th ch from hook and in each ch across (73 d c, counting turning ch as 1 d c). Ch 3, turn. Follow chart C to complete corner.

Cut linen 72 x 91 inches. Place insertion on top of linen and baste in place, taking care to have measurements of opposite sides correspond. Cut away excess linen at back of lace, allowing ½ inch on both sides of lace for turning under. Sew lace in place and make a neat hem on both sides. Place crocheted corners over corners of linen, ½ inch in from edges, and sew lace to linen as insertion was sewn. Make a narrow hem around all edges (this completes tablecloth). Cut eight napkins, each 18 inches square, and finish as for tablecloth.

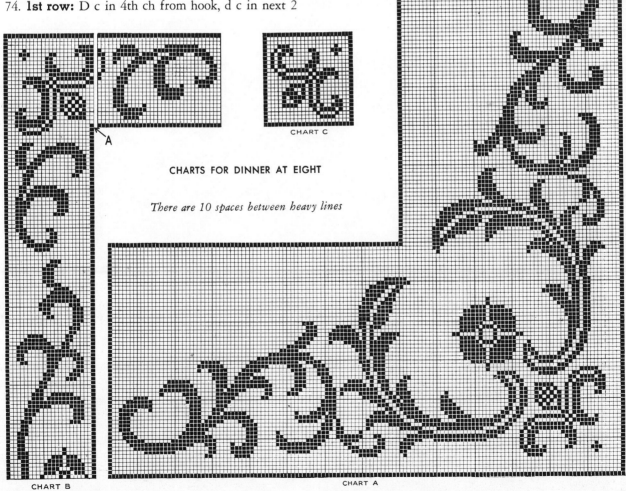

CHART C

CHARTS FOR DINNER AT EIGHT

There are 10 spaces between heavy lines

CHART B

CHART A

SPUN SUGAR

MADAME BUTTERFLY

Fragile lace spins into circles like spun sugar for your luncheon table.
For the rite of the tea table—butterflies and daisies help do the honors!

SPUN SUGAR

MATERIALS: Use one of the following threads in size 10, White or Ecru:

CLARK'S O.N.T. MERCERIZED CROCHET, *21 balls.*

J. & P. COATS MERCERIZED CROCHET, *15 balls.*

CLARK'S O.N.T. or J. & P. COATS BIG BALL BEST SIX CORD MERCERIZED CROCHET, *9 balls.*

MILWARD'S *steel crochet hook No. 9 or 10.*

Materials sufficient for a set consisting of centerpiece, 16½ inches in diameter; 4 plate doilies, 12½ inches; 4 bread and butter plate doilies, 9 inches; and 4 glass doilies, 5½ inches.

CENTERPIECE... Ch 6, join with sl st. **1st rnd:** Ch 3, 17 d c in ring. Join to 3rd st of ch-3. **2nd rnd:** Ch 5, skip 1 d c, * d c in next d c, ch 2, d c in next d c, ch 2, skip 1 d c. Repeat from * around, ending with ch 2, sl st in 3rd st of ch-5. **3rd rnd:** * Ch 10, d c in 4th ch from hook, (ch 1, skip 1 ch, d c in next ch) 3 times, s c in next d c, ch 10, s c in next d c. Repeat from * around, ending with ch 5, d tr in d c where first ch-10 started. **4th rnd:** * Ch 5, 3 tr in next sp (at tip), holding back the last loop of each tr on hook; thread over and draw through all loops, ch 1 to fasten (a cluster); ch 2, cluster, ch 2, cluster, ch 5, s c in next ch-10 loop. Repeat from * around, ending with ch 2, tr at tip of loop where first ch-5 started. **5th rnd:** * Ch 8, s c in sp preceding cluster; (ch 5, s c in next sp) 3 times. Repeat from * around. **6th rnd:** * 7 s c in next loop, 5 s c in next, 4 s c in next, 5 s c in next. Repeat from * around (126 s c). **7th rnd:** S c in each s c. **8th rnd:** Ch 3, d c in each s c. Join. **9th rnd:** Ch 5, * skip 1 d c, d c in next d c, ch 2. Repeat from * around; join (63 sps). **10th rnd:** * Ch 15, d c in 5th ch from hook; (ch 1, skip 1 ch, d c in next ch) 5 times; s c in next d c, ch 15, skip 3 sps, s c in next d c; ch 15, d c in 5th ch from hook; (ch 1, skip 1 ch, d c in next ch) 5 times; s c in next d c, ch 15, skip 4 sps, s c in next d c. Repeat from * around, ending with ch 8, tr tr where 1st ch-15 started. Join. **11th rnd:** Same as 4th rnd, making ch-8 before and after clusters, and ending rnd with ch 2, tr tr at tip of loop where 1st ch-8 started. **12th rnd:** Same as 5th rnd. **13th rnd:** Same as

(Continued on next page)

MADAME BUTTERFLY

MATERIALS: Use one of the following threads in size 20, White or Ecru:

CLARK'S O.N.T. MERCERIZED CROCHET, *30 balls.*

J. & P. COATS MERCERIZED CROCHET, *22 balls.*

CLARK'S O.N.T. or J. & P. COATS BIG BALL BEST SIX CORD MERCERIZED CROCHET, *13 balls.*

MILWARD'S *steel crochet hook No. 9 or 10.*

1 yd. linen, 36 inches wide.

GAUGE: 5 sps make 1 inch; 5 rows make 1 inch. Completed tea cloth measures about 54 inches square. Starting at bottom of chart, make a chain 72 inches long (15 ch sts to 1 inch). **1st row:** D c in 8th ch from hook; (ch 2, skip 2 ch, d c in next ch) 3 times— *4 sps made;* * d c in next 6 d c—*2 bls made;* 4 sps. Repeat from * 20 more times, 2 bls, 6 sps; (2 bls, 4 sps) 22 times. Cut off remaining chain. Ch 5, turn. **2nd row:** D c in next d c; (d c in next 2 ch, d c in next d c) twice—*2 bls made;* (4 sps, 2 bls) 21 times; 4 sps, 4 bls; (4 sps, 2 bls) 22 times, ch 2, skip 2 ch, d c in next ch. Ch 5, turn. **3rd row:** 1 sp, 10 bls, 248 sps, 10 bls, 1 sp. Ch 5, turn. **4th row:** 1 sp, ch 2,

(Continued on next page)

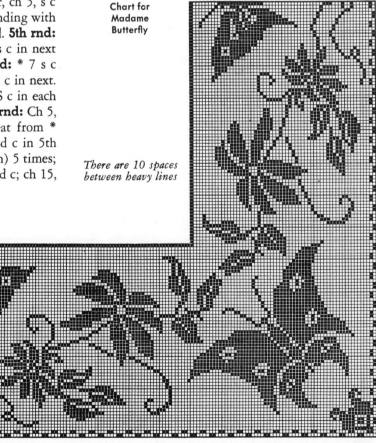

Chart for Madame Butterfly

There are 10 spaces between heavy lines

89

SPUN SUGAR

Continued

6th rnd (294 s c). **14th rnd:** Same as 7th rnd, increasing 3 s c in rnd (297 s c). **15th rnd:** Ch 3, d c in each st. Join. **16th rnd:** Ch 5, * skip 2 d c, d c in next d c, ch 3, skip 2 d c, d c in next d c, ch 2. Repeat from *; join. **17th to 22nd rnds incl:** Repeat 10th to 15th rnds incl. (462 s c in 20th rnd and 465 s c in 21st rnd). **23rd rnd:** Ch 5, * skip 2 d c, d c in next d c, ch 2, skip 2 d c, d c in next d c, ch 3, skip 2 d c, d c in next d c, ch 2. Repeat from *; join. **24th rnd:** * Ch 15, d c in 5th ch from hook; (ch 1, skip 1 ch, d c in next ch) 5 times; s c in next d c, ch 17, skip 4 sps, s c in next d c. Repeat from *; join. **25th rnd:** Same as 18th rnd, making ch-9 before and after clusters. **26th rnd:** Same as 19th rnd. **27th rnd:** Same as 20th rnd (651 s c). **28th rnd:** S c in each s c. Join. **29th rnd:** Ch 3, d c in each st. Join. **30th rnd:** Ch 5, * skip 2 d c, d c in next d c; (ch 2, skip 2 d c, d c in next d c) 3 times; ch 3. Repeat from *; join. Do not break off.

EDGING... 1st rnd: Sl st in next sp, ch 4 and complete a cluster, ch 3; in same sp make cluster, ch 3, cluster; * ch 6, skip 3 sps, s c in next d c, ch 6, skip 3 sps; in next sp make 3 clusters with ch-3 between. Repeat from * around, joining last ch-6 to tip of 1st cluster. **2nd rnd:** * In next 2 sps make 3 s c, ch 5, 3 s c; 6 s c in next 2 sps. Repeat from * around. Fasten off.

PLATE DOILY... Work as for centerpiece to 23rd rnd incl., but do not increase on the 21st rnd (462 s c). Then make edging as for centerpiece.

BREAD AND BUTTER PLATE DOILY... Work to 16th rnd incl., but do not increase on the 14th rnd (294 s c). Then make edging.

GLASS DOILY... Work to 9th rnd incl.; then make edging.

MADAME BUTTERFLY

Continued

skip 2 d c, d c in next 4 d c, 4 sps, 4 bls, 100 sps, 3 bls, 42 sps, 3 bls, 100 sps, 4 bls, 4 sps, 1 bl, 2 sps. Ch 3, turn. Chart shows ¼ of design. To make second half of each row, repeat the first half, starting at center and working back. Starting at 5th row, follow chart until 60 rows are made. Ch 5, turn. **61st row:** 17 sps, 1 bl, 11 sps, 3 bls, 1 sp, 6 bls, 6 sps, 4 bls, 10 sps, 1 bl. Ch 3, turn. Starting at 62nd row, follow chart to top; then reverse chart and work back to 62nd row incl. (149 short rows). Fasten off. Count 59 sps in from opposite side, attach thread to 4th d c of next bl and work to correspond, working back to 61st (not 62nd) row incl. (150 short rows). Do not break off, but ch 450 (15 ch sts to 1 inch) and complete 61st row at opposite side. Then follow chart to first row, working across chain. Fasten off.

Cut linen into a square to fit in center of lace, allowing for narrow hem. Hem linen. Sew to lace.

Flaunting colors as brilliantly gay as a gypsy's skirt, this merry little luncheon set follows the Romany pattern in its vivid border.

GYPSY TRAIL

MATERIALS: J. & P. Coats Knit-Cro-Sheen, *3 balls of Red, 3 balls of Green, 2 balls of Yellow and 2 balls of Black.*

Milward's *steel crochet hook No. 9.*

1 yd. of cotton crash, 50 inches wide.

Completed center mat measures about 14 x 36 inches; place mats measure about 12 x 18 inches.

CENTER MAT...Cut material 12 x 34 inches. Make a narrow hem all around. **1st rnd:** With Red, s c closely around edges, making 3 s c in each corner. Fasten off. **2nd rnd:** With Black, s c around, making 3 s c in center of 3 corner s c. Fasten off. **3rd rnd:** With Yellow, * s c in next 3 s c, skip 1 s c, insert hook at base of next st on previous row and complete as for an s c (long s c); insert hook at base of s c skipped on previous row and make a long s c; skip 2 s c behind the 2 long s c. Repeat from * around, increasing at corners. Fasten off. **4th rnd:** Attach Black and s c in each st, increasing at corners. Fasten off.

5th rnd: Attach Red and work as for 3rd rnd. **6th, 7th and 8th rnds:** Attach Green and repeat 4th rnd. **9th rnd:** With Yellow ** s c in next 3 sts, insert hook at base of next st on 3rd rnd below, * pull loop through, thread over, insert hook in same place. Repeat from * once more, pull loop through, thread over and pull through all loops on hook, skip s c behind this last st made and repeat from ** around, increasing at corners. Join. **10th rnd:** With Yellow, repeat 4th rnd. **11th rnd:** With Red, s c in next s c, * make a long s c, skip s c behind long s c, s c in next 3 sts. Repeat from * around, increasing at corners. Join. **12th rnd:** With Red, repeat 4th rnd. **13th and 14th rnds:** With Green, repeat 9th and 10th rnds. Fasten off. **15th and 16th rnds:** With Black, repeat 11th and 12th rnds. Fasten off at end of 16th rnd.

PLACE MATS...Cut 4 pieces of material, each 10 x 16 inches. Complete as for center mat.

SPRING SONG

For the luxurious atmosphere of an informal luncheon, this pattern of lacy motifs has an exquisite freshness and a precious jewel-like beauty.

SPRING SONG

MATERIALS: Use one of the following threads in size 30:

CLARK'S O.N.T. MERCERIZED CROCHET, *20 balls of White or Ecru, or 24 balls of any color.*

J. & P. COATS MERCERIZED CROCHET, *15 balls of White or Ecru, or 20 balls of any color.*

CLARK'S O.N.T. or J. & P. COATS BIG BALL BEST SIX CORD MERCERIZED CROCHET, *8 balls of White or Ecru, or 10 balls of any color.*

MILWARD'S *steel crochet hook No. 10 or 11.*

¾ yd. of linen, 36 inches wide, for napkins.

This amount is sufficient for 4 place mats, each about 12½ x 17½ inches, a center mat about 15 x 32½ inches, and 4 napkins, 12 inches square.

GAUGE: Each motif measures 2¼ inches square before blocking.

PLACE MATS (First Motif of First Strip) ... Starting at center, ch 9. **1st rnd:** In 9th ch from hook make d c, ch 5, d c, ch 5 and d c; (ch 2, skip 2 ch, in next ch make d c, ch 5 and d c) twice; (ch 2, skip 2 ch, d c in next st) twice. **2nd rnd:** Ch 9, 3-d tr cluster in 9th ch from hook—*to make a cluster, make 3 d tr, holding back the last loop of each d tr on hook; thread over and draw through all loops on hook, ch 1 tightly*—ch 3, sl st in ch-1 of cluster (p); ch 8, sl st at base of cluster, ch 12, turn. S c in p, ch 12, sl st at base of cluster, ch 1, turn. Over half of last ch-12 make 2 s c, 2 half d c and 6 d c; ch 8, s c in 4th ch from hook (p); ch 4, ch-4 p, ch 1, ch-4 p, * ch 7, 2-d c cluster in 5th ch from hook, ch-4 p in cluster, ch 4, sl st at base of cluster, ch 1, ch-4 p, ch 1, ch-4 p, ch 1, sl st in last d c made in ch-12; 6 d c over remaining 6 ch of same ch-12; 3 ch-4 p's with ch-1 between; ch 1, over next ch-12 make 12 d c, 2 half d c and 2 s c. Sl st at base of cluster, 2 s c in corner sp of center; in next sp make s c, ch-4 p and s c; 3 s c in corner ch-5, ch 9, 3-d tr cluster in 9th ch from hook, ch 4, sl st in cluster, ch 8, sl st at base of cluster, ch 12, turn. S c in p, ch 12, sl st at base of cluster, ch 1, turn. Over half of last ch-12 make 2 s c, 2 half d c and 6 d c; ch 4, ch-4 p, ch 4, s c in 7th d c down from top on last flower; 2 ch-4 p's with ch-1 between. Repeat from * around but, after the first 6 d c of last flower are made, make a sl st in 3rd ch from 1st p of first loop (thus joining last flower to first loop); complete flower. Fasten off.

Make another motif to within 3 p's between d c-groups of flower; make a ch-4 p, ch 2, sl st in cor-responding p of first motif, ch 2, sl st back in 1st ch of first ch-2 (thus second motif is joined to first). Complete rnd as before. Make 5 more motifs, joining in same way.

First Motif of Second Strip ... Work as for second motif of first strip, joining as before to first motif of first strip.

Second Motif ... Join to lower edge of first motif and to adjacent side of second motif of first strip.

Continue thus until there are 5 strips of 7 motifs.

FILL-IN LACE ... Ch 10, join with sl st. **1st rnd:** Ch 1, 20 s c in ring; sl st in ch-1. **2nd rnd:** Ch 1, s c in next s c, * ch 4, sl st in tip of free d c-cluster between joinings, ch 4, s c in next s c back on ring, s c in next 2 s c; (ch 1, p) 4 times; ch 6, sl st in 1st free p next to joining, ch 2, sl st in next free p on other side of joining, ch 5, skip 5 ch of ch-6, sl st in next ch; (ch-4 p, s c between next 2 p's) 3 times; ch-5 p, s c between next p and s c of ring, s c in same s c, s c in next 2 s c. Repeat from * 3 more times. Fasten off.

CENTER MAT ... Make 6 x 13 motifs.

Block pieces to measurements given.

NAPKINS (Make 4) ... Cut a 12½-inch square of linen, make a narrow hem. Place a motif over linen at one corner, and sew motif to linen. Cut away excess linen under motif, and hem.

SHINING HOUR

SHINING HOUR

MATERIALS: Use one of the following threads in
size 30:

CLARK'S O.N.T. MERCERIZED CROCHET, 75 *balls
of White or Ecru, or 90 balls of any color.*

J. & P. COATS MERCERIZED CROCHET, 56 *balls of
White or Ecru, or 75 balls of any color.*

CLARK'S O.N.T. or J. & P. COATS BIG BALL
BEST SIX CORD MERCERIZED CROCHET, 28 *balls
of White or Ecru, or 38 balls of any color.*

MILWARD'S *steel crochet hook No. 10 or 11.*

GAUGE: Each motif measures 4 inches in diameter
when blocked. For a tablecloth about 60 x 80
inches, make 15 x 20 motifs.

MOTIF...1st row: Ch 7, tr in 7th ch from hook;
* ch 2, tr in same place. Repeat from * until 11 sps
are made. Ch 2, sl st in 5th ch of ch-7. **2nd rnd:** Ch 1,
* in ch-2 sp make half d c, 3 d c, half d c; s c in tr.
Repeat from * around. **3rd rnd:** Sl st in each st to
2nd d c of next scallop, * ch 7, s c in center d c of
next scallop. Repeat from * 10 more times; ch 3, d c
in center d c of next scallop. **4th rnd:** * Ch 13, s c
in 3rd ch from hook, s c in next ch, half d c in next
2 ch, d c in next 3 ch, tr in next 3 ch, 4-tr cluster in
last ch—*to make cluster, make 4 tr, holding back the
last loop of each tr on hook; thread over and draw
through all loops on hook, ch 1 tightly.* Sl st in 4th
ch of next ch-7 loop. Repeat from * around, ending
with sl st at base of 1st cluster (12 points). Fasten off.
5th rnd: Attach thread to tip of 1st point, * ch 8,
s c in 4th ch from hook (p), ch 5, s c in tip of next
point. Repeat from * around. Join. **6th rnd:** Ch 1,
* roll the p of next loop over so that p points down
toward center of motif; then, working over ch at right
side of p, make 1 half d c, 3 d c, 2 tr; make 2 more tr,
holding back the last loop of each tr on hook; 2 tr
under ch at left of p, holding back the last loop of each
tr on hook; thread over and draw through all loops,
ch 4, sl st in tip of cluster; under same loop where

last 2 tr of cluster were made make 2 tr, 3 d c and
half d c; s c in next s c. Repeat from * around. Join
to ch-1. **7th rnd:** Ch 7, d tr in same place as sl st;
(ch 2, d tr in same place) 4 times. * S c in next p,
in s c between scallops make 6 d tr with ch-2 between.
Repeat from * around. Fasten off.

Make another motif to 6th rnd incl. **7th rnd:** Ch 7,
d tr in same place as sl st; (ch 2, d tr in same place)
4 times; s c in next p, * in s c between scallops make
3 d tr with ch-2 between; ch 1, sl st in corresponding
sp of fan on 1st motif, ch 1, d tr in same place as last
d tr on motif in work; (ch 2, d tr in same place as last
d tr) twice, s c in next p. Repeat from * once more.
Complete rnd as for 1st motif.

Join 2 points of each motif to 2 points of adjacent
motifs, leaving 1 fan free on each motif, between
joinings.

FILL-IN MOTIF... Ch 6, join with sl st. **1st rnd:**
Ch 5, * d c in ring, ch 2. Repeat from * until 7 sps
are made. Join last ch-2 to 3rd st of ch-5 (8 sps).
2nd rnd: Ch 7, d tr in same place as sl st, ch 2, d tr
in same place, * ch 1, sl st in free point of one motif,
ch 1, d tr back on fill-in motif. (Ch 2, d tr in same
place) twice; skip next d c, d tr in next d c; (ch 2,
d tr in same place) twice. Repeat from * around.
Fasten off.

For napkins, we suggest No. 1 on page 113.

TOP O' THE MORNING

QUEEN'S TASTE

MATERIALS: CLARK'S O.N.T. or J. & P. COATS MERCERIZED CROCHET, *size 50, 1 ball of White, Ecru, or any color.*

MILWARD'S *steel crochet hook No. 12 or 13.*

½ yd. linen, 18 inches wide.

GAUGE: 7 sps make 1 inch; 7 rows make 1 inch.

Completed tray mat measures 12½ x 17½ inches across center.

CORNERS (Make 4)... Starting at bottom of chart, ch 59. **1st row:** D c in 8th ch from hook, * ch 2, skip 2 ch, d c in next ch. Repeat from * until 13 sps are made, d c in next 6 ch (2 bls), ch 2, skip 2 ch, d c in next 7 ch. Ch 5, turn. **2nd row:** D c in 4th ch from hook, d c in next ch, d c in next d c, ch 2, skip 2 d c, d c in next, ch 2, skip 2 d c, d c in next d c, d c in next 2 ch, d c in next d c, 2 sps, 1 bl, 12 sps. Ch 5, turn. **3rd row:** 11 sps, 2 bls, 5 sps, d c in next 2 d c, foundation d c in 3rd st of turning ch—*to make a foundation d c, thread over, insert hook in ch and draw loop through; thread over and draw through one loop, thus making a chain st; thread over and complete as for a d c.* Make 2 more foundation d c by inserting hook in ch of previous d c, then make 1 d c in the usual way (1 bl increased). Ch 5, turn. **4th row:** 1 bl, 3 sps, 1 bl, 1 sp, 1 bl, 3 sps, 1 bl, 10 sps. Ch 5, turn. **5th row:** 10 sps, 1 bl, 3 sps, 3 bls, 3 sps, 1 bl, turn. **6th row:** Sl st in each of 4 d c (1 bl decreased), ch 3, 1 bl, 1 sp, 5 bls, 1 sp, 1 bl, 11 sps. Ch 5, turn. Starting at 7th row, follow chart to top to complete corner. Fasten off.

Cut linen 13 x 18 inches. Place corners over corners of linen, ½ inch in from edges; baste and sew in place. Cut away excess linen at back of lace, allowing ¼ inch for turning under. Hem neatly. Make a narrow hem all around edges.

MATERIALS: Use one of the following threads in size 30:

CLARK'S O.N.T. MERCERIZED CROCHET, *3 balls of White or Ecru, or 4 balls of any color.*

J. & P. COATS MERCERIZED CROCHET, *3 balls of White, Ecru or any color.*

MILWARD'S *steel crochet hook No. 10 or 11.*

GAUGE: Each motif measures about 3 x 3¾ inches across center. Completed tray mat measures about 11½ x 19 inches.

FIRST STRIP (First Motif)... Starting at center, ch 23, half d c in 6th ch from hook; (ch 1, skip 1 ch, d c in next ch) twice; (ch 1, skip 1 ch, tr in next ch) twice; (ch 1, skip 1 ch, d c in next ch) twice; ch 1, skip 1 ch, half d c in next ch, ch 2, sl st in last ch. Work is now done in rnds. **1st rnd:** Ch 1, 2 s c in same place as sl st, 2 s c in next sp, s c in next st; (s c in next ch-1, s c in next st) 7 times; 2 s c in ch-5, 3 s c in 3rd ch of same ch-5, 2 s c in same ch-5, s c in next st; (s c in next ch-1, s c in next st) 7 times; 2 s c in ch-5, sl st in 1st ch. **2nd rnd:** Ch 1, s c in next (end) s c; make a p as follows: ch 6, s c in 5th ch from hook; make 3 more p's, ch 13, remove hook, insert it in 2nd ch from last p made and draw loop of chain through; into loop just made make s c, half d c and 3 d c; ch 5, sl st in last d c—*a p made;* (3 d c in loop, p) 4 times; make 3 d c, half d c and s c in same loop, sl st at base of loop; (p, s c between next 2 p's) 3 times; ch-5 p, s c over next ch-1, sl st in last s c of oval, s c in same place as sl st, s c in next 2 s c; * (ch 1, p) 4 times, ch 13, remove hook, insert it in 2nd ch from last p made and draw last ch through; into loop just made make s c, half d c and 3 d c; sl st in last p of previous ch-13 loop; into second ch-13 loop make (3 d c, p) 4 times; make 3 d c, half d c and s c in same loop; sl st at base of loop; (ch-5 p, s c between next 2 p's) 3 times; ch-5 p, s c in next ch-1, between next p and oval; sl st in last s c of oval,

(Continued on next page)

QUEEN'S TASTE

Continued

s c in next 4 s c. Repeat from * 2 more times, but make 5 s c instead of 4 s c between p-loops. Make another p-loop, ending with 4 s c; make another p-loop, ending with 2 s c; make another p-loop, and work other half of rnd to correspond with first half, joining 1st and last p's of p-loop in order to complete joining of motif (12 loops in rnd). Fasten off.

Make another motif like this, joining the center p of center p-loop at one side to corresponding p of 1st motif.

Make 4 more motifs, joining as second was joined to first.

SECOND STRIP (First Motif) ... Work as for second motif of first strip, joining the 2nd and 3rd p's of 2nd p-loop to 6th and 7th free p's (counting from joining) on second motif of first strip; also joining 3rd and 4th p's of last p-loop to 6th and 7th free p's of first motif of first strip. Join last p to 1st p made, and complete rnd.

SECOND MOTIF ... Join to second and third motifs, as first motif was joined to first and second motifs; also join center p of center loop to corresponding p of first motif of second strip.

Continue in this manner until there are 5 motifs on 2nd strip. Make 5 more motifs for one more strip, alternating and joining them as before to opposite side of first strip. Fasten off.

Fill in all spaces between motifs as follows: Atach thread to center p of one free loop; (ch 8, s c in center p of next free loop) twice; ch 6, sl st in p where thread was attached. Fasten off.

EDGING ... Attach thread to center p-loop at one end of first strip. **1st rnd:** ** (Ch 20, s c in center p of next loop) twice; ch 20, tr in center p of next loop, tr in corresponding p of next motif; (ch 20, s c in center p of next loop) 5 times. * Ch 16, tr in center p of next loop, tr in corresponding p of next motif, ch 16, s c in center p of next loop; (ch 20, s c in center p of next loop) twice. Repeat from * 2 more times, ch 16, tr in center p of next loop, tr in corresponding p on next motif, ch 16, s c in center of next loop; (ch 20, s c in next loop) 4 times; ch 20, tr in center p of next loop, tr in corresponding p of next motif; (ch 20, s c in center p of next loop) 3 times. Repeat from ** once more. **2nd rnd:** Make 23 s c over each ch-20 loop, and 16 s c over each ch-16 loop. **3rd rnd:** Sl st in next 3 s c of 1st loop, ch 6; * (ch-5 p, ch 1, skip 2 s c, tr in next s c) 6 times; skip 2 s c of next loop, tr in next s c. Repeat from * once more; (ch-5 p, ch 1, skip 2 s c, tr in next s c) 5 times; tr in 6th s c of next loop; (p, ch 1, skip 2 s c, tr in next s c) 5 times; tr in 3rd s c on next loop. ** (P, ch 1, skip 2 s c, tr in next s c) 6 times; tr in 3rd s c on next loop. Repeat from ** 3 more times. **** (P, ch 1, skip 2 s c, tr in next s c) 3 times, tr in 5th s c of next loop; (p, ch 1, skip 2 s c, tr in next s c) 3 times; tr in 3rd s c of next loop; *** (p, ch 1, skip 2 s c, tr in next s c) 6 times; tr in 3rd s c of next loop. Repeat from *** once more. Then repeat from **** to within next corner and complete rnd to correspond with opposite end. Fasten off.

Stretch and pin mat right side down on ironing board, placing pins close together, around edge. Steam with hot iron and wet cloth. Press through a dry cloth until perfectly dry.

For napkins, we suggest No. 1 on page 113.

CRYSTAL WEB

MATERIALS: Use one of the following threads in size 30:

CLARK'S O.N.T. MERCERIZED CROCHET, 70 balls of *White or Ecru, or 89 balls of any color.*

J. & P. COATS MERCERIZED CROCHET, 52 balls of *White or Ecru, or 70 balls of any color.*

CLARK'S O.N.T. *or* J. & P. COATS BIG BALL BEST SIX CORD MERCERIZED CROCHET, 26 balls of *White or Ecru, or 35 balls of any color.*

MILWARD'S *steel crochet hook No. 10 or 11.*

GAUGE: Each motif measures 3½ inches square when blocked. Completed tablecloth measures about 60 x 80 inches.

MOTIF ... Starting at center, ch 7, join with sl st. **1st rnd:** 8 s c in ring; join. **2nd rnd:** * Ch 4, 3-tr cluster in same place as sl st—*to make cluster, make 3 tr, holding back the last loop of each tr on hook; thread over and draw through all loops on hook.* Ch 4, sl st in tip of cluster (a p made); ch 4, sl st at base of cluster, sl st in next s c. Repeat from * 7 more times; join. Fasten off.

DIAMONDS ... Starting at one end, ch 3. **1st row:** S c in 3rd ch from hook. Ch 2, turn. **2nd row:** 2 s c in s c. Ch 2, turn. **3rd row:** 2 s c in 1st s c, s c in next s c. Ch 2, turn. **4th row:** 2 s c in 1st s c, s c in each s c across. Ch 2, turn. Repeat 4th row until there are 13 s c in the row. Then make a sl st in p at tip of 1 petal of flower. Ch 1, turn. **Next row:** S c in each s c across. Ch 2, turn. **Following row:** Skip 1 s c, s c in each s c across. Ch 1, turn. Repeat the last row until 1 s c remains. **Next row:** S c in s c, * a long tr (thread over 5 times) in next p of next petal of flower; make another diamond as before. Repeat from * around, ending with a long tr, sl st in tip of first diamond. This completes 2nd rnd. **3rd rnd:** Ch 18, sl st in 5th ch from hook (a p made); ch 2, s c in center point of 1st diamond. ** Ch 1, p, ch 2, long tr in next long tr (between diamonds), * ch 1, p, ch 2, tr tr in same place as long tr. Repeat from * 6 more times, ch 1, p, ch 2, long tr in same place (a fan). Ch 1, p, ch 2, s c in center point of next diamond. Repeat from ** around, omitting last long tr of last fan; then sl st in 12th ch of ch-18 first made. Fasten off. This completes one motif.

Make another motif to within 3rd rnd. **3rd rnd:** Ch 18, sl st in 5th ch from hook, ch 2, s c in center point of 1st diamond. Ch 1, p, ch 2, long tr in next long tr, * ch 1, p, ch 2, tr tr in same place as long tr. Repeat from * 4 more times; ch 3, sl st in 4th p of first motif (counting from s c at center of diamond), ch 2, sl st in 3rd ch from sl st back on second motif; ch 2, tr tr in same place as last tr tr, ch 3, sl st in next p on first motif, ch 2, sl st in 3rd ch from sl st back on second motif, ch 2, tr tr in same place as last tr tr, ch 1, p, ch 2, long tr in same place, ch 1, p, ch 2, long tr in next long tr, ch 1, p, ch 2, tr tr in same place. Continue as for 3rd rnd of first motif, joining next 2 p's to 2 adjacent p's of first motif, and complete rnd.

Make 17 x 23 motifs, joining 4 p's of each motif to 4 p's of adjacent motifs, leaving 2 p's free on each motif between joinings. To eliminate rippled effect and achieve a smooth surface, block motifs carefully.

For napkins, we suggest No. 1 on page 113.

98

CRYSTAL WEB

The lovely design that made crochet history. A cloth of rare beauty that holds enchantment in its gossamer patterning. A charming background for those "special" occasions.

QUEEN ANNE'S LACE

MATERIALS: CLARK'S BIG BALL MERCERIZED CROCHET, *size 20, 20 balls of White or Ecru.*

MILWARD'S *steel crochet hook No. 8.*

GAUGE: Each motif measures about 4¾ inches in diameter.

Completed tablecloth measures about 60 x 80 inches.

FIRST STRIP (First Motif)... Ch 6, join with sl st. **1st rnd:** Ch 6, * tr in ring, ch 2. Repeat from * 6 times, ch 2, join to 4th st of ch-6 (8 sps). **2nd rnd:** Ch 4, 4 tr in 1st sp, * ch 2, 5 tr in next sp. Repeat from * around. Join last ch-2 to 4th st of ch-4. **3rd rnd:** Ch 4, tr in same place as sl st, tr in next 4 tr, * tr in 1st ch of ch-2, ch 3, tr in next ch of same ch-2, tr in next 5 tr. Repeat from * around. Join last ch-3 to 4th st of ch-4; sl st in 1st tr of group. **4th rnd:** Ch 4, tr in next 4 tr, working off together as for a cluster; * ch 4, 5 tr in next ch-3 sp, ch 4, skip 1st tr of next group, tr in next 5 tr, working off together as for a cluster. Repeat from * around. Join last ch-4 to tip of first cluster. **5th rnd:** Ch 8, * skip 1st 3 ch of ch-4, tr in next ch, tr in next 5 tr, tr in 1st ch of next ch-4, ch 4, tr in tip of cluster, ch 4. Repeat from * around. Join to 4th st of ch-8. **6th rnd:** * Ch 12, skip 1st tr of next group, tr in next 5 tr, working off together as for a cluster; ch 12, s c in the single tr between groups. Repeat from * around. Join last ch-12 to base of first ch-12 (16 loops). Break off.

SECOND MOTIF... Work as for first motif to 5th rnd incl. **6th rnd:** Ch 12, skip 1st tr of next group, tr in next 5 tr, working off together as for a cluster; ch 6, sl st in first ch-12 loop on first motif (always keep right side of work on top), ch 6, s c in next single tr on second motif, ch 6, sl st in next ch-12 loop on first motif, ch 6, make a cluster back on second motif. Complete this rnd as for first motif, with no more joinings.

Make 11 more motifs, joining in same manner (6 ch-12 loops free on each side of joinings on each motif), thus making a strip of 13 motifs.

SECOND STRIP (First Motif)... Work as for second motif of 1st strip and join as before to first motif of 1st strip, leaving 2 ch-12 loops free on first motif (counting from joining of 1st two motifs).

SECOND MOTIF... Work to 5th rnd incl. **6th rnd:** Work as for 6th rnd of previous motif, but join to the 3rd and 4th ch-12 loops (counting from joining) of second motif on 1st strip; then work 2 ch-12 loops back on motif in work, join to 3rd and 4th ch-12 loops of first motif of 2nd strip. Complete rnd with no more joinings (2 ch-12 loops are left free on each motif, to be joined later to fill-in motif). Work next 11 motifs of this strip thus, joining each motif to 2 adjacent motifs. Work 15 more strips.

FILL-IN MOTIF...1st rnd: Ch 8, tr in 8th ch from hook, ch 4, tr in same place, ch 4, tr in same place, ch 4, join to 4th ch of ch-8 (4 sps). **2nd rnd:** Ch 4, 6 tr in 1st sp, * ch 5, 7 tr in next sp. Repeat from * around, ch 5, join to 4th st of ch-4; sl st in 1st tr. **3rd rnd:** Ch 4, tr in next 4 tr, working off together as for a cluster, ch 5, join to 1st ch-12 loop of a large motif (as large motifs were joined), * ch 5, s c in next ch-4 loop back on fill-in motif, ch 5, join to 2nd ch-12 loop of same large motif, ch 5, work a 5-tr cluster back on fill-in motif, ch 5, join to 1st ch-12 loop of next large motif. Repeat from * around. Fasten off.

EDGING... Attach thread to joining point between any 2 large motifs. * 7 s c in 1st loop of next motif; in each remaining loop of same motif make s c, half d c, 5 d c, 4 tr, 5 d c, half d c, s c; 7 s c in last loop. Repeat from * all around tablecloth.

For napkins, we suggest No. 3 on page 113.

QUEEN ANNE'S LACE

Make a square a day for twelve days—join them together, that's the easy way to create a decorative cloth!

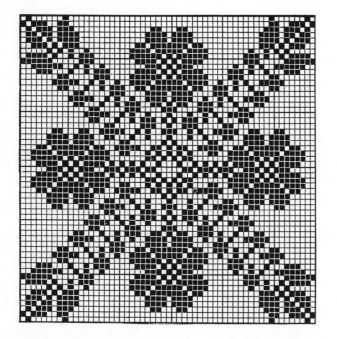

TRELLIS OF FLOWERS

MATERIALS: Use one of the following threads:

J. & P. Coats Knit-Cro-Sheen, *28 balls of White or Ecru, or 34 balls of any color.*

Clark's O.N.T. Lustersheen, *21 skeins of White or Ecru, or 28 skeins of any color.*

Milward's *steel crochet hook No. 7.*

Gauge: 3 sps make 1¼ inches; 3 rows make 1¼ inches. Each block measures about 23¾ inches square. Completed tablecloth measures about 73 x 97 inches.

BLOCK... Starting at center, ch 8, turn and make tr in 5th ch from hook and in each ch across. Work is now done in rounds. **1st rnd:** Ch 7; in same place as last tr make tr, ch 7 and tr; ch 3, skip 3 tr, tr at base of turning ch, ch 7, tr in same place as last tr, ch 3, tr in 4th ch, ch 7, tr in same place as last tr, ch 3, skip 3 tr, tr in next tr, ch 3, skip 3 ch, tr in next ch. **2nd rnd:** Ch 4, 3 tr over bar of last tr, tr in base of same tr, * ch 3, tr in next tr, 3 tr over next ch, tr in 4th st of same ch, ch 7, tr in same place as last tr, 3 tr over same ch, tr in next tr. Repeat from * around, ending with ch 3, tr in 4th st of ch-4 first made. **3rd rnd:** Ch 4, 3 tr over bar of last tr, tr in next ch, * ch 3, skip 3 tr, tr in next tr, 3 tr in next sp, tr in next tr, ch 3, skip 3 tr, tr in next tr, 3 tr in corner sp, tr in 4th ch of same corner, ch 7, tr in same place as last tr, 3 tr over corner ch, tr in next tr. Repeat from * around, ending with ch 3, tr in 4th st of ch-4 first made. **4th rnd:** Ch 4, 3 tr over bar of tr made, tr in next ch, tr in next 4 tr. * (Ch 3, tr in next 5 tr) twice,

3 tr in corner ch, tr in 4th st of same ch, ch 7, tr in same place as last tr, 3 tr in same corner, tr in next 5 tr. Repeat from * around, ending with ch 3, tr in 4th st of ch-4 first made. Starting with 5th rnd, follow chart until block is completed (the first sp of 5th rnd is indicated by an arrow on chart).

Make 3 x 4 blocks and sew them together on wrong side with neat over-and-over stitches.

EDGING...1st rnd: Attach thread to one tr, ch 4 and work tr in each tr and 3 tr in each sp all around, making 4 tr, ch 7 and 4 tr at corners. Join with sl st. **2nd and 3rd rnds:** Ch 4, tr in each tr around, making 4 tr, ch 7 and 4 tr in each corner. Fasten off.

We suggest a plain linen napkin, 18 inches square, for this cloth.

COCKTAIL CIRCLES

Lovely little doilies are a blessing to have around.

MATERIALS: Use one of the following threads in size 30:

CLARK'S O.N.T. MERCERIZED CROCHET, *3 balls of White or Ecru, or 4 balls of any color.*

J. & P. COATS MERCERIZED CROCHET, *3 balls of White, Ecru, or any color.*

CLARK'S O.N.T. *or* J. & P. COATS BIG BALL BEST SIX CORD MERCERIZED CROCHET, *2 balls of White, Ecru, or any color.*

MILWARD'S *steel crochet hook No. 10 or 11.*

Each small doily measures about 4 inches in diameter; large doily measures about 12½ inches in diameter.

SMALL DOILIES (Make 6) ...
Like motif No. 7190 (see page 13) to 6th rnd incl. **7th rnd:** Ch 9, s c in 4th ch from hook (a ch-4 p), * ch 1, d tr in same place as sl st, p. Repeat from * 3 more times. Ch 1, d tr in same place as last d tr, ch 3, s c in next p, ch 3, d tr in s c between scallops, (p, ch 1, d tr in same place as last d tr) 5 times. Continue thus around. Join last ch-3 to 5th st of ch-9 first made (12 fans). Fasten off.

LARGE DOILIES... Make 7 small doilies as before. Place 6 doilies to form a circle and sew together center p of 2 fans to center p of adjacent 2 fans with neat over-and-over stitches. Place remaining doily in center of circle and join center p of 2 fans to adjacent 2 p's of center doily, leaving 4 p's free between joinings.

SNOWDRIFT

Hundreds of small motifs drift together enchantingly to settle on your table with the white, bright beauty of a first snowfall.

MATERIALS:

CLARK'S O.N.T. *or* J. & P. COATS BIG BALL BEST SIX CORD MERCERIZED CROCHET, *size 50:*

Large Cloth—*32 balls of White or Ecru.*

Medium Cloth—*26 balls.*

Small Cloth—*21 balls.*

MILWARD'S *steel crochet hook No. 12 or 13.*

GAUGE: Each motif measures 1¾ inches in diameter.

MOTIF . . . Ch 10, join with sl st. **1st rnd:** Ch 3, 23 d c in ring. Join to 3rd st of ch-3. **2nd rnd:** Ch 4, * d c in next d c, ch 1. Repeat from * around. Join last ch-1 to 1st sp. **3rd rnd:** Ch 10, * skip 1 sp, tr in next sp, ch 6. Repeat from * around. Join last ch-6 to 4th st of ch-10. **4th rnd:** * Ch 2, skip 2 ch, d c in next ch, ch 2, d c in next ch, ch 2, s c in next tr. Repeat from * around; join. **5th rnd:** * Ch 2, d c in next d c, ch 2, d c in ch-2 sp, ch 2, d c in next d c, ch 2, s c in next s c. Repeat from * around. Fasten off.

Make another motif to 4th rnd incl. **5th rnd:** Ch 2, d c in next d c, * ch 1, sl st in corresponding sp on 1st motif, ch 1, d c in next sp on second motif, ch 1, sl st in next sp on 1st motif, ch 1, d c in next d c on second motif, ch 2, s c in next s c, ch 2, d c in next d c. Repeat from * once more; complete rnd as for 1st motif.

LARGE CLOTH . . . (70 x 86 inches). Join strips as follows: * 1 strip of 48 motifs, 1 strip of 49 motifs, joining 2 points of each motif to 2 points of adjacent motifs as before. Repeat from * 21 more times; add another strip of 48 motifs (45 strips in all).

MEDIUM CLOTH . . . (60 x 80 inches). Alternate 20 strips of 45 motifs with 19 strips of 46 motifs, as for large cloth.

SMALL CLOTH . . . (54 x 72 inches). Alternate 18 strips of 40 motifs with 17 strips of 41 motifs, as for large cloth.

For napkins, we suggest No. 3 on page 113.

CHATELAINE

Rich, lovely lace—a flattering foil for aristocratic settings! Lacy spokes join the interesting spinning wheels in an unusually charming sheer effect.

MATERIALS: Use one of the following threads in size 20, White or Ecru:

CLARK'S O.N.T. MERCERIZED CROCHET, 77 *balls.*

J. & P. COATS MERCERIZED CROCHET, 56 *balls.*

CLARK'S O.N.T. or J. & P. COATS BIG BALL BEST SIX CORD MERCERIZED CROCHET, 32 *balls.*

MILWARD'S *steel crochet hook No. 9.*

GAUGE: Each motif measures 4½ inches in diameter when blocked.

Completed tablecloth measures about 72 x 90 inches.

MOTIF...1st rnd: Starting at center, * ch 7, s c in 5th ch from hook (p). Repeat from * 7 more times. Join, having p's inside. **2nd rnd:** Ch 1 (3 s c between next 2 p's, s c at base of next p) 7 times, 3 s c between next 2 p's, sl st in 1st ch-1. **3rd rnd:** * Ch 20, d c in 9th ch from hook (ch 2, skip 2 ch, d c in next

(Continued on next page)

ch) 3 times, ch 2, s c where ch-20 started. Picking up only back loop, make s c in 4 s c. Repeat from * 7 more times (8 bars). Fasten off. **4th rnd:** Attach thread and make 4 s c in sp at top of bar, * ch 6, skip 1 sp of same bar, d tr in next sp, d tr in corresponding sp of next bar, ch 6, 4 s c in top sp of same bar. Repeat from * around, ending with 2 d tr, ch 6, sl st in 1st s c. **5th rnd:** Ch 1; picking up only back loop, make s c in 3 s c, * 7 s c in loop, s c between 2 d tr, 7 s c in next loop, s c in 4 s c. Repeat from *; join. **6th rnd:** Ch 8, (d tr in next s c, ch 4, d tr in same s c, ch 4) twice. Tr in next s c, ch 4, skip 7 s c, s c in next s c (1 fan); ch 4, skip 7 s c, tr in next s c, ch 4, and continue thus around. Join last ch-4 to 4th st of ch-8. **7th rnd:** Ch 1, * in ch-4 sp make half d c, 3 d c, and half d c; s c in next st. Repeat from * 4 more times, ch 3, s c in corresponding tr of next fan, and continue thus around. Fasten off.

Make another motif to 6th rnd incl. **7th rnd:** Ch 1; (in ch-4 sp make half d c, 3 d c and half d c; s c in next st) twice. * In next ch-4 sp make half d c and 2 d c; sl st in corresponding d c of fan on first motif; d c and half d c back in same ch-4 on second motif, s c in next st. Repeat from * once more, and continue as before, joining the 2nd and 3rd scallops of next fan to 2nd and 3rd scallops on first motif, and complete as for first motif.

Make 16 x 20 motifs, joining 4 scallops of each motif to 4 scallops of adjacent motifs, leaving 4 scallops free on each motif, between joinings.

FILL-IN LACE... Ch 1 loosely (this is center), * ch 14, 2-tr cluster in 7th ch from hook—*to make cluster, make 2 tr, holding back the last loop of each tr on hook; thread over and draw through all loops on hook, ch 1 to fasten*—ch 2, sl st in center d c of 1st free scallop to left of one joining, ch 2, sl st back in tip of cluster, ch 6, sl st at base of cluster, ch 9, cluster in 7th ch from hook, ch 2, sl st in center d c of 1st free scallop to right of joining, ch 2, sl st back in tip of cluster, ch 6, sl st in base of same cluster, ch 7, sl st in center. Repeat from * 3 more times. Fasten off.

For napkins, we suggest No. 1 on page 113.

ST. GEORGE and THE DRAGON

MATERIALS: CLARK'S O.N.T. or J. & P. COATS BIG BALL BEST SIX CORD MERCERIZED CROCHET, *size 20, White or Ecru, 41 balls.*

MILWARD'S *steel crochet hook No. 10.*

GAUGE: 5 sps make 1 inch; 5 rows make 1 inch.

Completed tablecloth measures 72 x 90 inches.

Starting at bottom of chart, make a chain 3 yds. long (15 ch sts to 1 inch). **1st row:** D c in 8th ch from hook, ch 2, skip 2 ch, d c in next ch (2 sps made); make 3 more sps, d c in next 24 ch (8 bls); * 10 sps, 8 bls. Repeat from * 8 more times, 5 sps. Cut off remaining chain. Ch 5, turn. **2nd row:** D c in next d c, d c in each of next 2 ch, d c in next d c (1 sp and 1 bl); make 3 more bls, ch 2, skip 2 d c, d c in next d c (1 sp); make 7 more sps, * 10 bls, 8 sps. Repeat from * across, ending with 4 bls, 1 sp. Ch 5, turn. Chart shows ¼ of design. To make second half of each row, repeat the first half, starting from center and working back. Follow chart until 5 rows are made. Ch 3, turn and follow chart until 26 rows are made. Ch 3, turn. **27th row:** 1 bl, 3 sps, 1 bl, 5 sps, 16 bls, 2 sps, 4 bls, 8 sps, 2 bls, 6 sps, 8 bls, 2 sps, 2 bls, 2 sps, 2 bls, 2 sps, 8 bls, 6 sps, ch 3, s c in next d c, ch 3, d c in next d c (1 lacet). Make 99 more lacets, and follow chart across. Ch 3, turn. **28th row:** 1 bl, 3 sps, 1 bl, 5 sps, 16 bls, 2 sps, 4 bls, 8 sps, 2 bls, 6 sps, 8 bls, 2 sps, 2 bls, 2 sps, 2 bls, 2 sps, 8 bls, 6 sps, ch 5; skip ch-3, s c and ch-3; d c in next d c (1 bar). Make 99 more bars, and follow chart across. Ch 3, turn. **29th row:** 1 bl, 2 sps, 1 bl, 8 sps, 4 bls, 2 sps, 10 bls, 12 sps, 2 bls, 8 sps, 6 bls, 2 sps, 6 bls, 2 sps, 8 bls, 6 sps, ch 3, skip 2 ch of bar, s c in next ch, ch 3, d c in next d c (lacet over bar). Make 99 more lacets, follow chart across. Ch 3, turn. Now follow chart to top; then reverse design by working back to 1st row. Fasten off.

We suggest a plain linen napkin, 18 inches square, for this cloth.

ST. GEORGE and
THE DRAGON

*There are 10 spaces
between heavy lines*

Chart for St. George and the Dragon

Dramatic—magnificent—the splendid design of this filet banquet cloth provides a regal setting for effects that are formal—for occasions that are stately.

There's a fresh bread-and-butter charm to this naïve luncheon set with china in its corners. The perfect setting for casual and country tables.

COUNTY FAIR

MATERIALS: J. & P. COATS KNIT-CRO-SHEEN, *9 balls of Blue and 1 ball of White.*
MILWARD'S *steel crochet book No. 6 or 7.*
This amount of materials is sufficient for 4 place mats, each about 12 x 17 inches, and a center mat, about 12 x 32 inches.
GAUGE: 10 d c make 1 inch; 4 rows make 1 inch. (1 square is equivalent to 3 d c.)
Before starting, divide White into 2 equal balls.

PLACE MATS... Starting at short side, with Blue ch 131 (to measure about 13 inches). **1st row:** D c in 4th ch from hook, d c in each ch across (129 d c, counting turning ch as 1 d c). Ch 3, turn. **2nd and 3rd rows:** D c in d c across. Ch 3, turn. **4th row:** D c in next 23 d c, leaving last 2 loops of last d c on hook; attach 1 ball of White and draw through the 2 loops. Holding Blue at top of previous row and working over it in order to conceal it, make

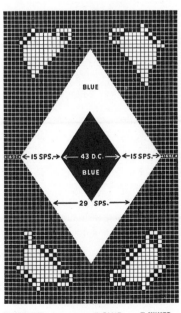

PLACE MAT   ■ BLUE   □ WHITE

COUNTY FAIR

Continued

d c in 3 d c, leaving last 2 loops of 3rd d c on hook; drop White, pick up Blue and draw through 2 loops on hook; then, holding White at top of previous row and working over it, make d c in 3 d c, drop White and continue to make d c in each of next 72 d c, leaving the last 2 loops of last d c on hook. Drop Blue, attach the 2nd ball of White and draw through 2 loops on hook; working over Blue, make d c in next 3 d c, leaving last 2 loops on hook. Drop White, pick up Blue and draw through 2 loops on hook; working over White, make d c in 3 d c; drop White. Carrying unused color over next 3 d c only, make d c in d c across, d c in 3rd st of turning ch. Ch 3, turn. Now follow chart, beginning at 5th row, until 9 rows are completed, concealing unused color as before and carrying it only so far as necessary to continue pattern on next row. **10th row:** 14 Blue d c, 21 White d c, 3 Blue d c, 3 White d c; carrying White over next 3 d c only, make 22 Blue d c, ch 1, skip 1

d c, d c in 22 d c, 3 White d c, 3 Blue d c, 21 White d c, 15 Blue d c. Ch 3, turn. **11th row:** Carrying unused color only so far as necessary, make 15 Blue d c (counting ch-3 as 1 d c), 18 White d c, 3 Blue d c, 3 White d c, 23 Blue d c, ch 1, skip 1 d c, d c in next d c, ch 1, d c in next d c, ch 1, skip 1 d c, d c in next 23 d c (1 sp increased at both sides of previous sp), 3 White d c, 3 Blue d c, 21 White d c, 15 Blue d c. Now follow chart until 24 rows are completed, always increasing 1 sp at both sides of sps of previous row, and breaking off White when design is completed (there should be 29 sps on 24th row). Ch 3, turn. **25th row:** D c in 35 d c, ch 1, skip 1 d c, d c in next d c, ch 1 and make 14 more sps, d c in next ch-1, d c in next d c, 15 sps, d c in each d c and in turning ch. **26th row:** 32 d c (counting ch-3 as 1 d c), 15 sps, d c in next ch-1, d c in next 3 d c, d c in next ch-1, d c in next d c (1 bl increased at both sides of bl of previous row), 15

sps, 32 d c. Ch 3, turn. Now follow chart until 35 rows are completed, always increasing 1 bl at both sides of bl of previous row (43 d c in center with 15 sps at both sides, on 35th row). **36th row:** D c in 13 d c, d c in next ch-1, d c in next d c (1 bl increased), 15 sps, 38 more d c, ch 1, skip 1 d c, d c in next d c (1 bl decreased at both ends of center d c-group), 15 sps, d c in next ch-1, d c in each d c across (another bl increased at inner edge). Ch 3, turn, and follow chart to top, decreasing 1 bl at both sides of center d c-group and increasing 1 bl at inner edge of outer d c-groups.

RUNNER... Work as for place mat until 60 rows are completed, omitting China designs at top. Then work rows of d c only, for 2 more inches. Continue with another diamond, finishing with China designs at top (see illustration).

SHEPHERDESS

As dainty as a Watteau shepherdess—this luncheon set with its filet center of delicate leaves fences in the design with a border of contrasting linen.

MATERIALS: Use one of the following threads in size 50:

CLARK'S O.N.T. MERCERIZED CROCHET, *18 balls of White or Ecru, or 21 balls of any color.*

J. & P. COATS MERCERIZED CROCHET, *13 balls of White or Ecru, or 18 balls of any color.*

MILWARD'S *steel crochet hook No. 12 or 13.*

2¼ yds. handkerchief linen, 36 inches wide.

This amount of materials is sufficient for 6 place mats, each about 12 x 18½ inches, and a center mat about 15½ x 34 inches.

GAUGE: 7 sps make 1 inch; 7 rows make 1 inch.

Chart

CENTER MAT... Starting at bottom of chart, make a chain 36 inches long (21 ch sts to 1 inch). **1st row:** D c in 8th ch from hook, ch 2, skip 2 ch, d c in next ch (2 sps), d c in next 3 ch (1 bl), ch 2, skip 2 ch, d c in next ch; make 8 more sps, * 1 bl, 9 sps, 1 bl, 5 sps, 1 bl, 9 sps. Repeat from * 6 more times, 1 bl, 9 sps, 1 bl, 2 sps. Cut off remaining chain. Ch 5, turn. **2nd row:** D c in next d c, ch 2, d c in next 4 d c; (2 d c in sp, d c in next d c) 4 times— *5 bls made—* 5 sps, 1 bl, 5 sps, 5 bls, 3 sps. This brings work to end of 2nd row on chart. Repeat 2nd row 7 more times, ending with 5 bls, 2 sps (thus finishing end of row to correspond with beginning). Starting at 3rd row, follow chart to top, always repeating design 7

more times and ending each row to correspond with beginning. When work reaches top row, reverse chart and work back to 1st row. Fasten off. Block this piece to measure 10½ x 29 inches.

Cut 2 strips of linen 5 x 34 inches, and 2 strips 5 x 16 inches. Double the 5-inch width to measure 2½ inches, and press fold. Sew together 2 short and 2 long strips to form an oblong, mitering all corners and making inner edges correspond with measurements of lace. Turn under the edges of linen, and sew neatly to edge of lace.

PLACE MATS... Starting at arrow on chart, ch 314 (21 ch sts to 1 inch). **1st row:** D c in 8th ch from hook, ch 2, skip 2 ch, d c in next ch; make 8 more sps, d c in next 3 ch; * 3 sps, 1 bl, 10 sps, 1 bl, 10 sps, 1 bl. Repeat from * across, ending with 10 sps. Ch 5, turn. **2nd row:** D c in next d c (sp-over sp), make 9 more sps, d c in next 3 d c (bl over bl), * 3 sps, 1 bl, 10 sps, 1 bl, 10 sps, 1 bl. Repeat from * across, ending with 10 sps. Ch 5, turn. Continue to top row of chart, always repeating design necessary number of times and ending rows to correspond with beginning. Then reverse chart and work back to arrow on chart. Fasten off. Block this piece to measure 8 x 14½ inches. Cut 2 strips of linen 5 x 19 inches, and 2 strips 5 x 13 inches. Finish as for center mat. This completes one place mat.

BALLERINA

Each motif spreads from its starlike center into a radiant pool—like the fluffy skirts of a ballerina—the whole interlaced with cobweb-fine lines.

MATERIALS:

CLARK'S BIG BALL MERCERIZED CROCHET, *size 20, White or Ecru, 30 balls.*

MILWARD'S *steel crochet hook No. 10.*

GAUGE: Each motif measures 5 inches in diameter.

Completed tablecloth measures about 70 x 90 inches.

MOTIF... Starting at center, ch 8, join with sl st. **1st rnd:** Ch 5, * d c in ring, ch 2. Repeat from * 6 more times. Join to 3rd st of ch-5 (8 sps). **2nd rnd:** Sl st in next sp, ch 5, 4 d tr in same sp, holding back the last loop of each d tr on hook; thread over and draw through all loops on hook (a cluster); * ch 8, 5 d tr in next sp, holding back the last loop of each d tr on hook; thread over and draw through all loops on hook (cluster). Repeat from * around, ending with ch 8, sl st at tip of 1st cluster made. **3rd rnd:** 10 s c in each sp (80 s c in rnd). **4th to 7th rnds incl:** S c in each s c, ending 7th rnd with sl st in next st. **8th rnd:** * Ch 5, skip 1 st, s c in next st, ch 5, skip 2 sts, s c in next st. Repeat from * around (32 loops). **9th rnd:** Sl st to center of next loop, 2 s c in loop, * ch 5, s c in next loop. Repeat from * 2 more times, ch 5, 2 s c in next loop, and continue thus around, ending with sl st in 1st s c made. **10th rnd:** Ch 1, s c in next 2 s c, * 2 s c in next loop; (ch 5, s c in next loop) twice, ch 5, 2 s c in next loop, s c in next 2 s c. Repeat from * around, ending with 2 s c in last loop, sl st in ch-1 first made. **11th rnd:** Ch 1, s c in next 4 s c, * 2 s c in next loop, ch 5, s c in next loop, ch 5, 2 s c in next loop, s c in next 6 s c. Repeat from * around, ending with sl st in ch-1 first made. **12th rnd:** Ch 1, s c in next 6 s c, * 2 s c in next loop, ch 7, 2 s c in next loop, s c in next 10 s c. Repeat from * around, ending rnd as before. **13th rnd:** Ch 1, s c in next 8 s c, * in ch-7 loop make 2 s c, ch 5, 2 s c; s c in next 14 s c. Repeat from * around. Join. **14th rnd:** Ch 1, s c in each s c, making 5 s c in each ch-5 loop. Join. **15th rnd:** Ch 1, s c in each s c, making 2 s c in center st of 5-s c group. Join. **16th rnd:** S c in next s c, ch 6 (to count as d c and ch-3), d c in same place as last s c, * ch 6, skip 5 s c, s c in next s c, ch 6; in center s c at tip of next point make d c, ch 3, d c; ch 6, skip 5 s c, s c in next s c, ch 6, skip 5 s c; in next s c make d c, ch 3, d c. Repeat from * around, joining last ch-6 to 3rd st of ch-6 first made. **17th rnd:** Sl st in next ch, s c in sp, ch 6, d c in same sp, * ch 6, s c in next s c, ch 7; in sp at point make d c, ch 3, d c; ch 7, s c in next s c, ch 6; in next sp make d c, ch 3, d c. Repeat from * around. Join and fasten off.

Make 14 x 18 motifs. With over-and-over stitches sew 3 points of one motif to corresponding 3 points of adjacent motifs, thus leaving 1 point free on each motif between joinings.

FILL-IN LACE... Ch 10, join to form ring. * Ch 11, sl st in a free point between joinings; ch 11, s c back in ring. Ch 16, sl st in joining; ch 16, s c in ring. Repeat from * 3 more times. Join and fasten off. Fill in all spaces between joinings in same manner.

For napkins, we suggest No. 3 on page 113.

AT YOUR FINGER TIPS . . . NEW IDEAS FOR NAPKINS

No. 1 . . . Make a 76-inch chain. **1st row:** S c in 11th ch from hook, * ch 6, skip 4 ch, s c in next ch. Repeat from * across (there should be a multiple of 3 loops). Ch 6, turn. **2nd row:** S c in 1st loop, * ch 4; 3 tr in next loop, holding back the last loop of each tr on hook; thread over and draw through all loops at once; ch 1 to fasten (a cluster). Ch 4, s c in 4th ch from hook (p); ch 1, in same loop make another cluster, p, ch 1, cluster, ch 4; s c in next loop, ch 2, p, ch 2, s c in next loop. Repeat from * across, ending with ch 3, d c at base of last loop. Fasten off.

Cut linen 18½ inches square. Make narrow hem all around. Sew edging to linen, easing in at corners.

No. 2 . . . Make a 76-inch chain. **1st row:** S c in 2nd ch from hook and in each ch across. Ch 5, turn. **2nd row:** Skip 2 s c, d c in next s c, * ch 2, skip 2 s c, d c in next s c. Repeat from * across, turn. **3rd row:** * Ch 3, d c in next d c, ch 3, sl st in top of d c just made (p); d c in same place as last d c, ch 3, s c in next d c. Repeat from * across. Fasten off.

Cut linen 18½ inches square. Make narrow hem all around. Sew edging to linen, easing in at corners.

No. 3 . . . Make a 76-inch chain. **1st row:** D c in 8th ch from hook, * ch 2, skip 2 ch, d c in next ch. Repeat from * across. Ch 1, turn. **2nd row:** * S c in d c, 2 s c in sp. Repeat from * across, ending with s c in 3rd ch following last d c. **3rd row:** * Ch 2, skip 7 s c, make 6 d tr with ch-2 between in next s c, ch 2, skip 7 s c, s c in next s c (a fan). Repeat from * across. Ch 2, turn. **4th row:** S c in 1st d tr of 1st fan; in next 5 sps make s c, half d c, 2 d c, half d c, s c (5 petals); s c in last d tr of same fan, ch 2, s c in 1st d tr of 2nd fan and make 5 petals; continue thus across. Fasten off.

Cut linen 18½ inches square. Make narrow hem all around. Sew edging to linen, easing in at corners.

These edgings make fine napkins to ensemble with your lace cloths.

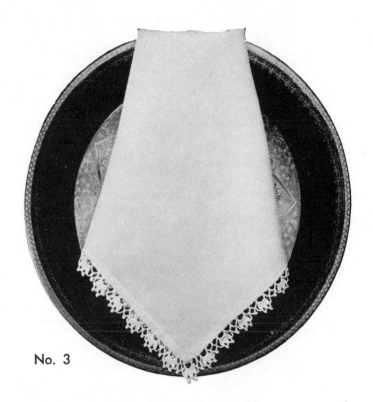

No. 3

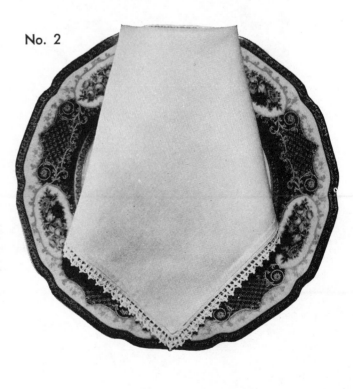

No. 2

No. 1

113

PINWHEEL *Table Cloth*

Materials: Clark's O.N.T. (60 balls) or J. & P. Coats (42 balls) Mercerized Crochet, size 50, White or Ecru.

Milward's steel crochet hook No. 12.

When completed, table cloth measures about 54 x 72 inches (18 x 24 blocks). 3-inch square blocks are made individually and joined to one another on the last round, as explained later.

First Block. Starting at center, ch 8, join with sl st to form ring. **1st rnd:** 16 s c in ring. **2nd rnd:** Ch 4 (to count as d c and ch-1), * d c in next s c, ch 1. Repeat from * around. Join last ch-1 with sl st to 3rd st of ch-4 first made (16 sps). **3rd rnd:** Ch 3, d c in same st as sl st, * ch 4, skip next d c, 2 d c in next d c. Repeat from * around. Join last ch-4 with sl st to 3rd st of ch-3 first made (8 groups of 2-d c). **4th rnd:** Sl st in next d c, ch 3 (to count as d c), * 2 d c in next loop, ch 5, skip 1st d c of next 2-d c group, d c in next d c of same group. Repeat from * around. Join last ch-5 with sl st to 3rd st of ch-3 first made. **5th rnd:** Sl st in next d c, ch 3 (to count as d c), d c in next d c, 2 d c in next loop, * ch 6, skip 1st d c of next d c-group, d c in each of next 2 d c of same group, 2 d c in next loop. Repeat from * around. Join last ch-6 with sl st as before. **6th rnd:** Sl st in next d c, ch 3 (to count as d c), d c in each of next 2 d c, 2 d c in next loop, * ch 7, skip 1st d c of next d c-group, d c in each of next 3 d c of same group, 2 d c in next loop. Repeat from * around. Join last ch-7 with sl st as before. **7th, 8th and 9th rnds:** Continue in this manner, always skipping the 1st d c of each d c-group and making 2 increases in each d c-group, also on 7th rnd making ch-8 loops; on 8th rnd, ch-9 loops; on 9th rnd, ch-10 loops (8 d c in each group on 9th rnd). Join with sl st. **10th rnd:** Sl st in each of next 2 d c, ch 3 (to count as d c), d c in each of next 5 d c, * ch 6, s c in next loop, ch 6, skip 1st 2 d c of next d c-group, d c in each of next 6 d c, ch 10, s c in next loop, ch 10, skip 1st 2 d c of next d c-group, d c in each of next 6 d c, repeat from * around. Join with sl st. **11th rnd:** Sl st in each of next 2 d c, ch 3, d c in each of next 3 d c, * ch 7, s c in next loop, s c in following loop, ch 7, skip 1st 2 d c of next d c-group, d c in each of next 4 d c, ch 6, 4 d c in next loop, ch 10, 4 d c in next loop, ch 6, skip 1st 2 d c of next d c-group, d c in each of next 4 d c. Repeat from * around. Join with sl st. **12th rnd:** Sl st in each of next 2 d c, ch 3, d c in next d c, * ch 11, s c between the 2-s c of previous rnd, ch 11, skip 1st 2 d c of next d c-group, d c in each of next 2 d c, ch 7, 4 d c in next loop, ch 7, 4 d c in next loop, ch 11, 4 d c in same loop (this is corner), ch 7, 4 d c in next loop, ch 7, skip 1st 2 d c of next d c-group, d c in each of next 2 d c. Repeat from * around. Join with sl st. Break off.

Second Block. Work as for First Block to 11th rnd incl. **12th rnd:** Sl st in each of next 2 d c, ch 3, d c in next d c, ch 11, s c between the 2-s c of previous rnd, ch 11, skip 1st 2 d c of next d c-group, d c in each of next 2 d c, ch 7, 4 d c in next loop, ch 7, 4 d c in following loop, ch 5, s c in corner loop of First Block (always keeping right side of work on top), ch 5, 4 d c in same loop back on Second Block, ch 3, s c in next ch-7 loop of First Block, ch 3, 4 d c in next loop on Second Block, ch 3, s c in next loop on First Block, ch 3, skip 1st 2 d c of d c-group on Second Block and make d c in each of next 2 d c, ch 5, s c in next ch-11 loop on First Block, ch 5, s c between the 2-s c on Second Block, ch 5, s c in ch-11 loop on First Block, ch 5, skip 1st 2 d c of d c-group on Second Block and make d c in each of next 2 d c, ch 3, s c in next loop on First Block, ch 3, 4 d c in next loop back on Second Block, ch 3, s c in next loop on First Block, ch 3, 4 d c in next loop on Second Block, ch 5, s c in corner loop on First Block, ch 5, 4 d c in same loop on Second Block, ch 7, 4 d c in next loop on Second Block. Continue this rnd as in First Block with no more joinings. Break off. Make 23 more blocks, joining each block to previous one as Second Block was joined to First Block, making a strip of 24 blocks.

Make second strip as follows:

First Block of Second Strip. Work as for Second Block of first strip and join, as before, to First Block alongside of first strip. **Second Block.** Work as before to 11th rnd incl. **12th rnd:** Work as for 12th rnd of previous blocks, but join to the two adjacent blocks and complete rnd. Work next 22 blocks of this strip joining thus to adjacent two blocks. Make 16 more strips of blocks and join as before.

Edging. 1st rnd: Attach thread to ch-7 loop just before a corner, ch 11, s c in corner loop, ch 15, s c in same corner loop, * ch 11, s c in next loop. Repeat from * around, making a ch-15 loop at each corner as before. **2nd rnd:** Sl st in each of 3 ch sts of next loop, 5 s c in same loop, ch 7, d c in corner loop, ch 3, d c in same loop, ch 7, * 5 s c in next loop, ch 5, d c in next loop, ch 3, d c in same loop, ch 5. Repeat from * around, making corners as before. **3rd rnd:** S c in each of 4 s c of 5-s c group, ch 6, 4 s c in next loop, ch 6, d c in corner ch-3 sp, ch 3, d c in same sp, ch 6, 4 s c in next loop, * ch 6, s c in each of 4 s c of next 5-s c group, ch 6, d c in ch-3 sp, ch 3, d c in same sp. Repeat from * around, making corners as before. **4th rnd:** S c in each of 3 s c of 4-s c group, ch 7, s c in each of 3 s c of 3-s c group, ch 7, d c in corner ch-3 sp, ch 3, d c in same sp, ch 7, s c in each of 3 s c of 3-s c group, * ch 7, s c in each of 3 s c of 4-s c group, ch 7, d c in ch-3 sp, ch 3, d c in same sp. Repeat from * around, making corners as before. **5th rnd:** S c in center s c of 3-s c group, ch 8, s c in center of next s c-group, ch 8, in corner ch-3 sp make 4 d c with a ch-5 p between d c's (3 p's), ch 8, s c in center of next s c-group, * ch 8, s c in center of next s c-group, ch 8, in next ch-3 sp make 4 d c with ch-5 between d c's. Repeat from * around, making corners as before. Break off.

TRELLIS *Luncheon Set*

Materials: Clark's O.N.T. (14 balls) or J. & P. Coats (10 balls) Mercerized Crochet, size 30, White or Ecru.

Milward's steel crochet hook No. 10.

1-1/3 yds. of 72-inch wide linen.

When completed cloth measures 48 inches square and 4 napkins, each 12 inches square.

Cut linen 48 inches square for cloth and 12 inches square for each of 4 napkins.

Cloth. Triangle Insert: Ch 12, join with sl st to form ring. Hereafter, the right side of work is always facing you. Do not turn at end of rows. **1st row:** 4 s c in ring, ch 2, 4 s c in ring, ch 2, 2 s c in ring. **2nd row:** Ch 12, remove hook and draw loop under ch-2, 4 s c in ch-12, ch 7, remove hook and draw loop under next ch-2 (top of loop), 4 s c in ch-7, ch 2, 4 s c in same ch-7 (thus filling top of second square). Ch 2, 4 s c in ch-12, ch 2, 2 s c in same ch-12. **3rd row:** Ch 12, remove hook and draw loop under 1st ch-2, 4 s c in ch-12. Ch 7, draw loop under next ch-2, 4 s c in ch-7, then ch 7, draw loop under last ch-2, 4 s c, ch 2, 4 s c in same ch-7. Ch 2, 4 s c in next ch-loop. Ch 2, 4 s c in ch-12, ch 2, 2 s c in ch-12. **4th row:** Ch 12, continue to increase until 27 rows are made. On last ch-12 make: 4 s c, ch 2, 5 s c, ch 2, 4 s c, ch 2. In each loop along base of triangle work 4 s c and ch 2. Fasten and break off. Make 3 more triangle inserts.

Triangle Corner: Ch 12, join with sl st to form ring. **1st row:** Work 4 s c, ch 2, 4 s c in ring. The right side of work is always facing you. Do not turn at end of rows. Ch 7, remove hook and draw loop under ch-2, 4 s c in ch-7, ch 2, 4 s c in same ch-7. Ch 7, remove hook and draw loop under ch-2, 4 s c in ch-7. Ch 2, 4 s c in same ch-7. Ch 2, across top of row work: 4 s c, ch 2, 4 s c, ch 2, 4 s c, ch 2, 2 s c. **2nd row:** Ch 12, remove hook and draw loop under 1st ch-2, 4 s c in ch-12, ch 7, remove hook and draw loop under next ch-2, 4 s c in ch-7. Ch 7, remove hook and draw loop under next ch-2, 4 s c in ch-7, ch 7, remove hook and draw loop under next ch-2, 4 s c in ch-7, ch 9, remove hook and draw loop under ch-2 which is just before 4 s c just made (to form scallop at the top), 4 s c in ch-9, ch-4 p, 4 s c in ch-9, p, 4 s c in ch-9, then across top of row work: ch 2, 4 s c, ch 2, 4 s c, ch 2, 4 s c. Ch 2, over ch-12 work: 4 s c, ch 2, 2 s c. **3rd row:** Ch 12, remove hook and draw loop under 1st ch-2, 4 s c in ch-12, ch 7, remove hook and draw loop under next ch-2, 4 s c in ch-7, ch 7, remove hook and draw loop under next ch-2, 4 s c in ch-7, ch 7, remove hook and draw loop under next ch-2, 4 s c in ch-7, ch 7, remove hook and draw loop under next ch-2, 4 s c in ch-7, ch 2, 4 s c in same ch-7. Then across top of row work: ch 2, 4 s c, ch 2, 4 s c, ch 2, 4 s c, ch 2. Over ch-12 work: 4 s c, ch 2, 2 s c. **4th row:** Ch 12, remove hook and draw loop under 1st ch-2, 4 s c in ch-12, * ch 7, remove hook and draw loop under next ch-2, 4 s c in ch-7. Repeat from * 4 more times. Ch 9 (for scallop), and complete it as in 2nd row. Then across top of row work as before, ch 2, 4 s c and so on. Continue to widen in this manner, until 16 scallops are made. Work next row across as before but in the last ch-12 work only ch 2 and 4 s c (thus omitting the ch 2 and 2 s c in order to stop increasing). Ch 12, work across as before, but coming back in last ch-12 work ch 2 and 4 s c (again omitting the ch 2 and 2 s c), ch 12. Thus work back and forth without increasing until the row which makes the 17th scallop is made; but coming back on this row, make 17 scallops to correspond with the other side (the first scallop of this row forming one of the two scallops at corner). After the 17th scallop is completed on this row, there will be 3 sps across in a short row which will form the beginning of the edging. Work over these 3 sps as follows: Ch 2, 4 s c in next sp, ch 2, 4 s c in next sp, ch 2, 4 s c in next sp. This completes Corner Triangle both sides of which should measure the same. If not, pull in place as s c's slip easily on the ch's. Do not break off. Place this Triangle Corner over linen so that it fits exactly into the corner, and pin in place at base of triangle. Cut away linen underneath triangle, allowing 3/4 inch to make a hem. Take away pins and cut the other three corners to correspond. Then make a 1/2 inch hem all around linen. Continue for edging over the 3 sps as follows:

Edging. 1st row: Ch 12, remove hook and draw loop under ch-2, 4 s c in ch-12, ch 7, remove hook and draw loop under next ch-2, 4 s c in ch-7, ch 7, remove hook and draw loop under next ch-2, 4 s c in ch-7, ch 2, 4 s c in same ch-7, ch 2, 4 s c in next sp, ch 2, 4 s c in next sp. **2nd row:** Ch 12, remove hook and draw loop under ch-2, 4 s c in ch-12, ch 7, remove hook and draw loop under next ch-2, 4 s c in ch-7, ch 7, remove hook and draw loop under next ch-2, 4 s c in ch-7, ch 9 (for scallop), complete scallop and work over the next 2 sps as before, in the last sp make ch 2 and 4 s c, ch 12 and continue thus back and forth without increasing and making a scallop in every other row until edging measures the same as one side of linen. Now begin increasing for another triangle corner as the previous one, and thus work around.

Sew crochet work around linen, with over-and-over stitches. Place one Triangle Insert in center of each side, 3 inches in from edge of linen (as in illustration). Sew with over-and-over stitches. Cut away linen underneath triangle, leaving 1/2 inch for finishing and make a hem on wrong side.

Napkin. Make a 1/2 inch hem all around napkin. Work edging as for triangle corner but having only 2 sps instead of 3 sps.

REGENT *Dinner Cloth*

Materials: Clark's O.N.T. (60 balls) or J. & P. Coats (45 balls) Mercerized Crochet, size 30, White or Ecru.

Milward's steel crochet hook No. 11.

2 yds. of 18-inch wide linen.

When completed, tablecloth measures about 60 x 80 inches, and 4 napkins, each about 14 inches square. Lace is made in 3 individual pieces then sewed to linen, as explained later.

Gauge: 6 sps make 1 inch; 6 rows make 1 inch. For satisfactory results, it is important to get gauge as specified. The chart on page 120 shows ¼ of the design.

Outer Lace: Starting at center of narrow edge of cloth, (see "A-A" on chart), ch 114 (to measure about 6½ inches), turn. **1st row:** D c in 9th ch from hook, d c in each of next 45 d c (15 bls made). Ch 2, skip 2 ch, d c in next ch (1 sp made), make 3 more sps, 4 bls, 2 sps, 2 bls, 2 sps, 2 bls. Ch 3, turn. **2nd row:** D c in each of next 6 d c, make 2 sps, then ch 2, skip 2 d c, d c in next d c, d c in each of next 3 d c, 2 d c in sp, d c in next d c, 2 d c in next sp, d c in each of next 4 d c, ch 2, skip 2 d c, d c in next d c, make 3 more sps, 4 bls, 4 sps, 12 bls, 1 sp, 2 bls. Ch 3, turn. **3rd row:** 1 bl, 1 sp, 1 bl, 4 sps, 7 bls, 4 sps, 4 bls, 6 sps, 2 bls, 4 sps, 2 bls. Ch 3, turn. Hereafter follow chart from 4th row on to 120th row incl (see "B-B" on chart). At end of 120th row, ch 59, turn.

121st row: D c in 9th ch from hook, and continue making 51 more sps, then 2 bls. Ch 3, turn. Continue to work until "C-C"; then ch 5, turn and continue, still following chart to "D-D" to complete corner, ending with 2 rows of d c (174 rows). At end of 174th row, do not break off but ch 3, and continue for strip on other side as follows: **Next row:** Work 6 d c across bars of next 2 d c, ch 2, and make 34 sps across, working along end of rows ("C-D"). **Following row:** 3 sps, 2 bls, 29 sps, 2 bls. Ch 3, turn. Hereafter follow chart. When row reaches to the top row, reverse the design, by working back from the top row to "C-D". Then ch 59, turn and work to "B-D". Then continue along ends of rows from "B-B" until you reach "A-A". Then reverse the design by working back from "A-A" to "B-B". This completes 2½ sides. Complete remainder to correspond. Sew the two ends together.

Inner Lace: Starting at bottom, ch 725 (to measure about 41½ inches), turn. **1st row:** D c in 9th ch from hook, make 2 bls, 1 sp, 13 bls, 3 sps, 5 bls, 190 sps, 5 bls, 3 sps, 13 bls, 1 sp, 2 bls, 1 sp. Ch 3, turn. **2nd row:** 3 bls, 1 sp, 12 bls, 4 sps, 4 bls, 192 sps, 4 bls, 4 sps, 12 bls, 1 sp, 3 bls, ch 3, turn. Hereafter follow chart as far as "O". Then, working on one side, follow chart to top row. Break off. Work other side to correspond. Make another piece same as this. Sew pieces together.

Center Lace: Starting at short end, ch 75, turn. **1st row:** D c in 6th ch from hook, make 23 more sps. Ch 5, turn. **2nd and 3rd rows:** Sp over sp of previous row. Ch 5, turn. **4th row:** 5 sps, 2 bls, 10 sps, 2 bls, 5 sps. Ch 5, turn. **5th row:** 4 sps, 4 bls, 8 sps, 4 bls, 4 sps. Ch 5, turn. **6th row:** 3 sps, 2 bls, 2 sps, 2 bls, 6 sps, 2 bls, 2 sps, 2 bls, 3 sps. Ch 5, turn. Hereafter follow chart to the top row; then reverse the design by working back to the 1st row.

Cut linen into strips, each 3½ inches wide, making 2 each of the following lengths: 62½ inches, 40½ inches, 26½ inches, 4½ inches; and four 3½-inch squares. Make a ¼-inch hem all around linen strips, and sew to lace strips as in illustration.

STARTING HERE CH 725

STARTING HERE CH 114

CHART FOR REGENT

MEXICANA *Luncheon Set*

Materials: Clark's O.N.T. Mercerized Crochet, size 10, 2 balls of Sport Green, 6 of Spanish Red, 4 of Dk. Orange, 2 of Black, and 1 ball of Steel Blue, size 30; or J. & P. Coats Mercerized Crochet, 2 balls of Sport Green, 5 balls of Spanish Red, 3 balls of Dk. Orange, 2 balls of Black and 1 ball of Steel Blue.

Milward's steel crochet hook No. 6.

1½ yds. 54-inch width ecru linen.

This material is sufficient for four place mats, each about 12 x 18 inches, and a center mat about 14 x 26 inches.

Place Mat. Cut linen 11 x 17 inches and make a narrow hem. **1st row:** Attach Sport Green along one edge and work s c closely all around over hem. Join with sl st and break off. **2nd row:** Attach Spanish Red, ch 5, thread over, ** skip 2 s c, insert hook in next st and draw loop through, * thread over, insert hook in same st and draw loop through. Repeat from * once more (7 loops on hook), then thread over hook and draw through all loops on hook, (thus a group-st is made), ch 2. Repeat from ** around, making 2 group-sts at each corner st. Join last group with sl st to 3rd st of ch-5 first made. Break off. **3rd row:** Attach Black and make 3 s c in each ch-2 sp. Join with sl st and break off. **4th row:** Attach Dk. Orange and work as for 2nd row, but taking care to have group-sts come directly over those of previous row, making 2 group-sts at each corner. Join with sl st and break off. Repeat the 3rd and 4th rows alternately, using Steel Blue for 5th row, Spanish Red for 6th row, Sport Green for 7th row, Dk. Orange for 8th row, Spanish Red for 9th row. Fasten all threads securely.

Center Mat. Cut linen 13 x 25 inches, and work exactly as for Place Mat.

COBWEB DOILY *Luncheon Set*

Materials: Clark's O.N.T. (8 balls) or J. & P. Coats (6 balls) Mercerized Crochet, size 50, White.

Milward's steel crochet hook No. 10.

This material is sufficient for a set to serve four. Each set consists of a plate doily—10 inches, bread and butter plate doily—8 inches, and a glass doily—7 inches in diameter.

Plate Doily. Ch 7, join with sl st to form ring. **1st rnd:** Ch 6, * d c in ring, ch 3, repeat from * until 7 sps are made; then, ch 3, join with sl st (8 sps). Every rnd is joined with a sl st unless otherwise specified. **2nd rnd:** Ch 7, 4 d c in next sp, * ch 4, 4 d c in next sp. Repeat from * around, ending rnd with 3 d c in last sp. Join to 3rd st of ch-7 first made. **3rd rnd:** In each ch-4 loop make petals as follows: 1 s c, 1 half d c, 3 d c, 1 half d c, 1 s c, making ch-6 between petals. After last petal is made, ch 3, d c at base of 1st petal made. **4th rnd:** * Ch 8, 1 s c in next ch-6 loop. Repeat from * around. **5th rnd:** In each loop work: 1 s c, 1 half d c, 9 d c, 1 half d c, 1 s c. **6th rnd:** Ch. 13, * 1 d c between 2 petals of previous row, ch 11. Repeat from * around. Join in 3rd st of ch-13 first made. **7th rnd:** In each loop work: 1 s c, 1 half d c, 11 d c, 1 half d c, 1 s c. **8th rnd:** Ch 16, * 1 d c between next 2 petals of previous row, ch 13. Repeat from * around. Join last ch-13 with sl st to 3rd ch of ch-16 first made. **9th rnd:** In each loop make: 1 s c, 1 half d c , 15 d c, 1 half d c, 1 s c. **10th rnd:** Sl st to 1st d c of next petal, * ch 5, skip 2 d c, tr in next d c, ch 5, skip 2 d c, s c in next d c, ch 3, skip 1 d c, s c in next d c, ch 5, skip 2 d c, tr in next d c, ch 5, skip 2 d c, s c in next d c, ch 5, s c in 1st d c of next petal. Repeat from * around, ending with ch 3, d c at base of 1st loop made. **11th rnd:** Sl st to center of 2nd loop, * ch 5, tr in next loop, ch 5, s c in next loop, ch 3, s c in next loop. Repeat from * around. Skip loops over which sl st is made, s c in next ch-5 loop, ch 3, s c in next loop. **12th to 22nd rnds incl:** Repeat from * of 11th rnd and work around and around, making 1 ch more in every large loop in every other rnd. After last tr is made in 22nd rnd, ch 5, s c in next loop, ch 3, s c in same loop. Break off. **23rd rnd:** Attach to center of ch-3 loop, ch 4, make a 3-tr cluster in same loop. ** Ch 19, d c in 5th ch from hook, * ch 2, skip 2 ch, d c in next ch. Repeat from * 4 more times. 1 cluster in same place as last cluster, ch 10, make 2 clusters with ch-5 between in next tr, ch 10, make 1 cluster in next ch-3 loop. Repeat from ** around and break off. **24th rnd:** Attach thread to ch-5 between clusters, ch 10, * 1 d tr in 3rd d c up from cluster, ch 5, skip 1 d c, tr in next d c, ch 5, s c in turning ch, ch 5, tr in d c opposite last tr, ch 5, d tr opposite last d tr, ch 5, d tr in next ch-5 between clusters, ch 5. Repeat from * around. Join last ch-5 to 5th st of ch-10 first made. **25th rnd:** ** Ch 5, 3 s c in next ch-5, * in each of next 2 ch-5's make: 1 s c, 1 half d c, 4 d c, 1 half d c, 1 s c, ch 3; then repeat from * once more.

3 s c in ch-5, ch 5. Repeat from ** around. Join last ch-5 with sl st to 1st s c made. Break off. **26th rnd:** Attach to ch-3 at top of any point. Ch 11, * 1 tr tr in ch-5 at base of point, ch 5, sl st in 5th ch from hook, 1 tr tr in same place as tr tr just made, ch 9, turn, 7 tr tr with ch-3 between each tr tr in ch-5 ring just formed. Ch 3, s c in 7th ch of ch 11. Ch 1, turn, and make 1 s c in each ch-3 with ch-5 between s c's (7 loops). Ch 4, 1 s c in ch-3 loop at top of point, ch 12. Repeat from * around and fasten off.

Bread and Butter Plate Doily. Work as for Plate Doily to 11th rnd incl. **12th to 17th rnds incl:** Repeat from * of 11th rnd and work around and around. After last tr is made in 17th rnd, ch 5, s c in next loop, ch 3, s c in same loop. Break off. **18th rnd:** Attach to center of ch-3 loop, ch 4, make a 3-tr cluster in same loop. ** Ch 18, d c in 4th ch from hook, * ch 2, skip 2 ch, d c in next ch. Repeat from * 4 more times. 1 cluster in same place as last cluster, ch 5, make 2 clusters with ch-4 between in next tr, ch 5, make 1 cluster in next ch-3 loop. Repeat from ** around and break off. **19th rnd:** Attach thread to ch-4 between clusters, ch 7, * 1 d tr in 3rd d c up from cluster, ch 5, skip 1 d c, tr in next d c, ch 5, 1 s c in turning ch, ch 5, 1 tr in d c opposite last tr, ch 5, d tr opposite last d tr, ch 2, d tr in next ch-4 between clusters, ch 2. Repeat from * around. Join last ch-2 to 5th st of ch-7 first made. **20th rnd:** **Ch 2, 2 s c in next ch-2, * in each of next 2 ch-5's make: 1 s c, 1 half d c, 4 d c, 1 half d c, 1 s c, ch 3; then, repeat from * once more, 2 s c in ch-2. Repeat from ** around. Join last ch-2 with sl st to 1st s c made. Break off. **21st rnd:** Attach to ch-3 at top of any point. Ch 9, * 1 tr tr in ch-3 at base of point, ch 5, sl st in 5th ch from hook, 1 tr tr in same place as tr tr just made, ch 8, turn, 7 d tr with ch-3 between each d tr in ch-5 just formed. Ch 1, s c in 6th ch of ch-9. Ch 1, turn, and make 1 s c under each ch-3 with ch-4 between s c's (7 loops). Ch 3, 1 s c in ch-3 loop at top of point, ch 9. Repeat from * around and join. Break off.

Glass Doily. Work as for Plate Doily to 4th rnd incl. **5th rnd:** Same as 7th rnd of Plate Doily. **6th rnd:** Sl st to 1st d c of next petal, * ch 5, skip 1 d c, tr in next d c, ch 5, skip 1 d c, s c in next d c, ch 3, skip 1 d c, s c in next d c, ch 5, skip 1 d c, tr in next d c, ch 5, skip 1 d c, s c in next d c, ch 5, 1 s c in 1st d c of next petal. Repeat from * around, ending with ch 3, d c at base of first loop made. **7th to 10th rnds incl:** Repeat from * of 11th rnd of Plate Doily, and work around and around. After last tr is made in 10th rnd, ch 3, s c in next loop, ch 3, s c in same loop. Break off. **11th rnd:** Attach to center of ch-3 loop, ch 4, make a 3-tr cluster in same loop. ** Ch 18, d c in 4th ch from hook, * ch 2, skip 2 ch, 1 d c in next ch. Repeat from * 4 more times. 1 cluster in same place as last cluster, ch 3, make 2 clusters with

(continued on next page)

COBWEB DOILY

Continued

ch-5 between in next tr, ch 5, make 1 cluster in next ch-3 loop. Repeat from ** around and break off. **12th rnd:** Attach thread to ch-5 between clusters, ch 7, * tr in 3rd d c from cluster, ch 5, skip 1 d c, d c in next d c, ch 5, 1 s c in turning ch, ch 5, d c in d c opposite last d c, ch 5, tr opposite last tr, ch 2, tr in next ch-5 between clusters, ch 2. Repeat from * around. Join last ch-2 in 5th st of ch-7 first made. **13th rnd:** ** 2 s c in next ch-2, * in each of next 2 ch-5's make: 1 s c, 1 half d c, 4 d c, 1 half d c, 1 s c, ch 3; then repeat from * once more. 2 s c in

ch-2, ch 2. Repeat from ** around. Join last ch-2 with sl st to 1st s c made. Break off. **14th rnd:** Attach to ch-3 at top of any point. Ch 9, * 1 tr tr in ch-3 at base of point, ch 5, sl st in 5th ch from hook, 1 tr tr in same place as tr tr just made, ch 8, turn, 7 d tr with ch-3 between each d tr in ch-5 just formed. Ch 1, s c in 6th ch of ch-9. Ch 1, turn, and make 1 s c under each ch-3 with ch 4 between s c's (7 loops). Ch 3, 1 s c in ch-3 loop at top of point, ch 9. Repeat from * around. Join and break off.

CLIMBING ROSE *Table Cloth*

Materials: Clark's O.N.T. (34 balls) or J. & P. Coats (28 balls) Mercerized Crochet, size 20, White or Ecru

Milward's steel crochet hook No. 10.

5 yds. of 36-inch width linen.

When completed, tablecloth measures about 60 x 68 inches, and 8 napkins each about 15½ inches square. Strips of lace are made, and then flowers are made and appliqued. Cut strips of linen, being sure to cut on straight of goods (not bias), each 4½ inches wide and according to length specified on Diagram B. Make a ¼ inch hem on long sides of long linen strips

—A—

and along all edges of No. 1 and No. 11 corner pieces. Cut a piece of paper measuring about 60½ x 68 inches. Pin each linen strip in place on paper as in Diagram A. Now trim short ends of linen strips leaving ¼ inch for hem. Remove from paper and hem edges.

First Lace Strip. Starting at short end, ch 83 (to measure about 6½ inches), turn. **1st row:** 1 d tr in 10th ch from hook, 1 d tr in next ch, * ch 5, skip 4 ch, 1 d tr in each of next 2 ch. Repeat from * across (12 sps and ½ sp). Ch 2, turn. **2nd row:** * S c in each of next 2 d tr, ch 5. Repeat from * across, ending row with 1 s c in each of last 2 d tr. Ch 8, turn. **3rd row:** Skip 1st 2 s c and ch-5, * make 1 d tr in each of next 2 s c, ch 5. Repeat from * across, ending row with 1 d tr in each of last 2 s c. Then, ch 10, make 1 d tr in same place as d tr just made. Ch 4, turn (11 sps and ½ sp on each end). **4th row:** S c in each of 4th and 5th sts of ch-10, * ch 5, s c in each of next 2 s c. Repeat from * across, ending row with 1 s c in each of last 2 d tr. Ch 8, turn. These last 2 rows constitute the pattern. Repeat these 2 rows until lace strip measures 14½ inches along 1 edge, ending with the d tr-row and omitting the last ch-10 and the last d tr. Then, ch 2, turn. To decrease, work as follows: **Next row:** S c in each of 1st 2 d tr, * ch 5, s c in each of next 2 d tr. Repeat from * across, ending row as usual. Ch 8, turn. **Following row:** Work as for 3rd row, ending row with 1 d tr in each of last 2 d tr. Ch 2, turn. Repeat these last 2 rows until only the ½-sp remains. Break off. This completes the 1st lace strip. Make remaining strips to correspond, following measurements on Diagram A. Sew lace strips and linen strips alternately in position, inconspicuously.

Appliqued Flowers.

Flower: Starting at center, ch 7, join with sl st to form ring. **1st rnd:** Ch 5 (to count as tr and ch-1), make 19 tr with ch-1 between each tr. Join last

124

ch-1 with sl st to 4th st of ch-5 first made. **2nd rnd:** Make s c in each tr and in each ch-1 sp (39 s c). **3rd rnd:** * Ch 3, tr in each of next 3 s c, ch 3, s c in next s c (1 petal made). Repeat from * around (10 petals in all). Break off. **Leaf:** Starting along center, ch 25, turn. **1st row:** S c in 2nd ch from hook and s c in next ch, 1 half d c in next ch, d c in each of next 5 ch, d tr in each of next 8 ch, d c in each of next 5 ch, 1 half d c in next ch, d c in each of last 2 ch, ch 3, turn. Repeat this row on other side of foundation ch. Break off. Make 3 more leaves. This completes 1 group. Make 40 groups and sew to lace strips as in Diagram A.

Napkins. Cut linen into eight 16-inch squares, as in Diagram B. Make a narrow hem all around.

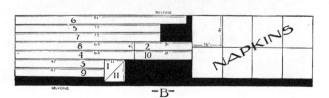

MOSAIC
Table Cloth

Materials: Clark's O.N.T: (68 balls) or J. & P. Coats (51 balls) Mercerized Crochet, size 30. Milward's steel crochet hook No. 11.

When completed, tablecloth measures 54 x 72 inches. 252 individual octagonal blocks, each about 3¾ inches from side to side, are made, then sewed together.

Block. Starting at center, wind thread 12 times around tip of forefinger, thus forming ring. **1st rnd:** Make 40 s c in ring. Join with sl st. **2nd rnd:** Ch 8 (to count as d c and ch-5), * skip 4 s c, d c in next s c, ch 5. Repeat from * around. Join last ch-5 with sl st to 3rd st of ch-8 first made (8 sps). **3rd rnd:** Ch 3 (to count as d c), 6 d c in next sp, * ch 2, 7 d c in next sp. Repeat from * around. Join last ch-2 with sl st to 3rd st of ch-3 first made. **4th rnd:** Ch 3, d c in each of next 6 d c, * ch 3, d c in each of next 7 d c. Repeat from * around. Join as before. **5th rnd:** Sl st in next d c, ch 3, d c in each of next 4 d c, * ch 5, s c in next sp, ch 5, skip 1 d c, d c in each of next 5 d c. Repeat from * around. Join last ch-5 with sl st as before. **6th rnd:** Sl st in next d c, ch 3, d c in each of next 2 d c, * ch 5, s c in next loop, 4 d c in s c between the 2 loops, s c in next loop, ch 5, skip 1st d c of next d c-group, d c in each of next 3 d c. Repeat from * around. Join last ch-5 with sl st. **7th rnd:** Sl st in next d c, ch 3, d c in next d c, * ch 5, s c in next loop, 4 d c in next s c, s c in center of next 4-d c group, 4 d c in next s c, s c in next loop, ch 5, skip 1 d c of 3-d c group, d c in each of next 2 d c. Repeat from * around. Join as before. **8th rnd:** Sl st across to center of next loop, * ch 7, s c in center of next 4-d c group, 4 d c in next s c (which is between the 2 groups), s c in center of next 4-d c group, ch 7, s c in next loop, ch 7, skip 2 d c, s c in next loop. Repeat from * around. Join last ch-7 with sl st to base of 1st loop. **9th rnd:** Sl st across to center of loop, * ch 7, s c in center of next 4-d c group, ch 7, s c in next loop, ch 7, s c in next loop, ch 7, s c in next loop. Repeat from * around. Join as before. **10th rnd:** Sl st across to center of loop, * ch 7, s c in next loop. Repeat from * around. Join as before (32 loops). **11th rnd:** Sl st across to center of loop, * ch 4, s c in next loop, ch 4, 4 d c in next loop, ch 4, 4 d c in same loop, ch 4, s c in next loop, ch 4, s c in next loop. Repeat from * around. Join and break off. This completes one block. Make 252 blocks.

To Join Blocks: Place blocks in position (14 x 18 blocks). With over-and-over stitches sew one side of one block (from ch-4 between d c-groups to ch-4 between next d c-groups) to corresponding side of the adjacent block (always having wrong side of work on top). (See stitch detail). Then fill in spaces left open by motifs as follows: **Fill-in-Lace. 1st rnd:** Attach thread to 3rd s c on one block (counting from right to left), * ch 9, skip joining of 2 blocks, s c in 1st s c on adjacent block, ch 9, skip next s c of same block, s c in next s c. Repeat from * around (8 loops in all). See stitch detail. **2nd rnd:** Sl st across to center of loop, * ch 9, s c in next loop. Repeat from * around. Join with sl st to base of 1st loop. **3rd rnd:** Sl st across to center of loop, * ch 3, s c in next loop. Repeat from * around. **4th rnd:** 2 s c in each loop and 1 s c in each s c. Join and break off. Fill in all remaining spaces in same way.

DETAIL

DAFFODIL *Luncheon Set*

Materials: Clark's O.N.T. (22 balls) or J. & P. Coats (16 balls) Mercerized Crochet, size 30, White or Ecru.

Milward's steel crochet hook No. 11.

This material is sufficient for 4 place mats, each about 12 x 18 inches and a center mat about 12 x 36 inches. Flowers are made individually and then sewed to mats.

Gauge: 7 sps make 1 inch; 7 rows make 1 inch.

Starting at one end, ch 75 (to measure about 4 inches), turn. **1st row:** D c in 6th ch from hook, * ch 2, skip 2 ch, d c in next ch. Repeat from * across (24 sps). Row should measure about 3½ inches. Ch 5, turn. **2nd row:** Skip ch-2, d c in next d c, * ch 2, d c in next d c. Repeat from * across. Ch 5, turn. Repeat 2nd row, thus making sp over sp until piece measures 2½ inches. Break off. Make another piece same as this, but with 1 additional row. Do not break off but ch 104 (to measure about 6 inches), then continue making sp over sp across first piece.

Ch 5, turn. Work in pattern until piece measures 4 inches from deepest point.

To start shaping, work as follows: **Next row:** Sl st across first 17 sps (or across first 2½ inches), ch 5, continue in pattern to within 17 sps (or 2½ inches) from end. Ch 5, turn. Work in pattern over these center sps for 10 more inches. Then ch 51 (to measure about 3 inches). Break off. Attach thread to opposite end of same row, ch 53 (to measure about 3 inches), turn. **Following row:** D c in 6th ch from hook, * ch 2, skip 2 ch, d c in next ch. Repeat from * across chain, continue across center sps and continue across other chain making 17 sps. Ch 5, turn. Work in pattern for 1½ inches. Then work over the first 24 sps, making sp over sp for 2½ inches. Break off. Attach thread to opposite side and work to correspond. Attach thread to one corner, ch 3, and work a row of d c closely together all around edges, making 5 d c in each outer corner and skipping the 2 corner sps at inner corners. Join and break off.

Flowers. Starting at center, ch 15, join with sl st to form ring. **1st rnd:** Ch 1, 30 s c in ring. **2nd rnd:** S c in each of next 6 s c. Ch 1, turn. Then work as for 2nd row, increasing 1 s c at end of each row until there are 14 s c in the row. Then decrease 1 s c at both ends of each row until 2 s c remain. Then sl st in each of 2 s c. Fasten and break off. Work remaining 4 petals in same way. Tack petals together with needle and thread. Make 12 flowers and sew in place as in illustration.

Center Mat. Work exactly as for Place Mats, but making the center section 27½ inches long (instead of 10 inches). Make 26 flowers and sew in place as in illustration.

GARDEN FERN

Luncheon Set

Materials: Clark's O.N.T. (15 balls) or J. & P. Coats (11 balls) Mercerized Crochet, size 50, White or Ecru.

Milward's steel crochet hook No. 10.

This material is sufficient for 4 place mats, each about 11 x 17 inches, and a center mat about 14 x 25 inches. Motifs measure about 2¾ inches in diameter. They are made individually, then sewed together. **Motif.** Starting at center, ch 9, join with sl st to form ring. **1st rnd:** Ch 3 (to count as d c), 23 d c in ring. Join with sl st to 3rd st of ch-3 first made. **2nd rnd:** Ch 3, d c in next d c, * ch 3, skip next d c, d c in each of next 2 d c. Repeat from * around. Join last ch-3 with sl st to 3rd st of ch-3 first made. **3rd rnd:** Ch 3, 2 d c in next d c, * ch 5, d c in next d c, 2 d c in next d c. Repeat from * around, joining last ch-5 with sl st to 3rd st of ch-3 first made. **4th rnd:** Ch 3, * 2 d c in next d c, d c in next d c, ch 6, d c in 1st d c of next d c-group. Repeat from * around. Join with sl st as before. **5th rnd:** Ch 3, * 2 d c in each of next 3 d c, ch 7, d c in 1st d c of next d c-group. Repeat from * around (7 d c in each d c-group). Join as before. **6th rnd:** Ch 3, d c in each of next 3 d c, * ch 2, d c in same place as d c just made, d c in each of next 3 d c, ch 8, d c in each of next 4 d c. Repeat from * around. Join as before. **7th rnd:** Sl st in each st to within ch-2 sp, sl st in sp, ch 6 (to count as d tr and ch-1), work 6 d tr in ch-2 sp with ch-1 btween each d tr, * ch 4, s c in next ch-8 loop, ch 4, 7 d tr in next ch-2 sp

with ch-1 between each d tr. Repeat from * around. Join last ch-4 with sl st to 5th st of ch-6 first made.

8th rnd: Sl st in next ch-1 sp, * ch 3, s c in next sp. Repeat from * 4 more times, then ch 3, s c in next ch-4 loop, ch 3, s c in next s c, ch 3, s c in next ch-4 loop, ch 3, s c in next ch-1 sp, and repeat thus around. Join and break off. This completes one motif. Make 24 motifs.

To Join Motifs: Place motifs in position (4 x 6 motifs). With over-and-over stitches, sew the 2 ch-3 loops of one motif (those directly over the 2nd and 3rd d tr) to the corresponding 2 ch-3 loops of the adjacent motif (always having right side of work on top). See stitch detail. Then fill in spaces between motifs as follows: **Fill-in-lace.** Starting at center, ch 9, join with sl st to form ring. **1st rnd:** Ch 3 (to count as d c), 23 d c in ring. Join with sl st. **2nd rnd:** Ch 8, sl st to one motif in 3rd loop (counting from right to left of a joining), * ch 8, s c in each of next 3 d c back on fill-in-lace, ch 8, skip next 4 ch-3 loops of same motif, sl st in next loop, ch 8, s c in each of next 3 d c back on fill-in-lace ch 8, sl st in 3rd ch-3 loop on next motif. Repeat from * around. Join and break off.

Center Mat. Work exactly as for place mats, but having 5 x 9 motifs.

If desired, starch slightly and press.

OCCASIONAL DOILY

Materials: Clark's O.N.T. (2 balls) or J. & P. Coats (1 ball) Mercerized Crochet, size 50.

Milward's steel crochet hook No. 11.

When completed, doily measures about 12 inches in diameter.

Starting at center, ch 10, join with sl st to form ring. **1st rnd:** Ch 4 (to count as 1 tr), make 31 tr in ring. Join with sl st. **2nd rnd:** * Ch 5, skip 1 tr, s c in next. Repeat from * around (16 loops). Sl st in 3 sts of first loop. **3rd rnd:** * Ch 13, s c in next loop. Repeat from * around. **4th rnd:** * 7 s c in next loop, ch 3, 1 p (to make a p, ch 4 and sl st in 4th ch from hook), ch 3, 1 p, ch 1, 1 p, ch 3, 1 p, ch 3, 7 s c in same loop. Repeat from * around. Break thread. **5th rnd:** Attach thread to ch-1 between 2 p's at top of loop of previous rnd. Ch 12 (to count as 1 d c and ch-9), * d c in ch-1 of next loop, ch 9. Repeat from * around. Join last ch-9 with sl st to 3rd ch of first ch-12. **6th rnd:** Ch 6 (to count as 1 d c and ch-3), 1 d c in same place as sl st, * ch 3, d c in 5th st of ch-9, ch 3, d c in same place, ch 3, d c in next d c, ch 3, d c in same place. Repeat from * around. Join last ch-3 to 4th st of ch-7.
7th rnd: Ch 4 (to count as 1 tr), tr in ch-3, ch 3, 2 tr in same ch-3, * ch 3, skip ch-3, in next ch-3 make: 2 tr, ch 3, 2 tr. Repeat from * around. Join last ch-3 to 4th st of ch-4 first made. Sl st in next 2 sts to bring work to ch-3. **8th rnd:** Ch 3, in same ch-3 sp make: * 2 tr, 1 d tr, 2 tr, 1 d c, ch 3; 1 s c in next ch-3, ch 3, 1 d c in next ch-3. Repeat from * around. Join last ch-3 with sl st to 1st ch-3 made. Sl st to d tr. **9th rnd:** Ch 15 (to count as 1 d tr and ch-9), * d tr in d tr of next scallop, ch 9. Repeat from * around. Join last ch-9 to 6th st of 1st ch-16. **10th rnd:** 11 s c in each ch-9. **11th rnd:** * Ch 3, 1 p, ch 5,

1 p, ch 3, s c in 5th s c of 11-s c loop, ch 3, 1 p, ch 5, 1 p, ch 3, 1 s c in d tr. Repeat from * around (66 loops). Join last ch-3 to 1st st of 1st ch-3. Sl st across 5 sts (to 3rd ch between 2 p's). **12th to 18th rnds incl:** Same as 11th rnd, but putting s c's in ch-5's between the 2 p's of each loop, ending as before. **19th rnd:** * Ch 6, a 3 d tr-cluster in ch-5 between 2 p's of next loop (for a 3 d tr-cluster, make 3 d tr, holding back on hook the last loop of each d tr—4 loops on hook—then work off loops on hook 2 at a time), ch 5, a 3 d tr-cluster in same place, ch 5, a 3 d tr-cluster in same place, ch 6, s c in ch-5 between 2 p's of next loop, ch 3, 1 p, ch 5, 1 p, ch 3, s c in ch-5 between 2 p's of next loop. Repeat from * around, ending with 1 s c in sl st first made. Sl st in next 8 sts to bring work to 1st st of ch-5 after cluster of next group. **20th rnd:** Ch 6, complete a cluster in same ch-5, * ch 5, a cluster in same ch-5, ch 5, a cluster in next ch-5, ch 5, a cluster in same place, ch 9, s c in ch-5 between 2 p's of next loop, ch 9, a cluster in ch-5 after 1st cluster of next group. Repeat from * around. Join last ch-9 to 6th st of 1st ch-6. Sl st 2 sts. **21st rnd:** Ch 6, complete a cluster in same ch-5, ** ch 2, 1 p, ch 2, a cluster in same place, * ch 2, 1 p, ch 2, a cluster in next ch-5, ch 2, 1 p, ch 2, a cluster in same place. Repeat from * once more. Ch 5, then work as follows: Thread over 3 times, insert hook in 6th st of next ch-9, pull loop through, thread over, and work off 2 loops on hook (4 loops left on hook), thread over, insert hook in 4th st of next ch-9, pull loop through, then take off 2 loops at a time 5 times, ch 5, make a cluster in next ch-5 after 1st cluster of next group. Repeat from ** around, joining last ch-5 to 1st cluster made. Break off.

VENETIAN DOILY

Materials: Clark's O.N.T. or J. & P. Coats Mercerized Crochet, 1 ball, size 50, White or Ecru.

Milward's steel crochet hook No. 11.

When completed, doily measures about 7 inches in diameter.

Starting at center, ch 6, join with sl st to form ring. **1st rnd:** Ch 7 (to count as 1 tr and ch-2), * tr in ring, ch 2. Repeat from * until 19 sts are made; then, ch 2, join with sl st to 5th st of ch-6 first made (20 sps). **2nd and 3rd rnds:** * Ch 5, s c in next loop. Repeat from * around. **4th rnd:** Sl st to center of next loop, ch 10 (to count as 1 tr and ch-5), * tr in next loop, ch 5. Repeat from * around. Join with sl st to 5th ch of ch-9 first made. **5th rnd:** Sl st in next st, ch 5 (to count as 1 d c and ch-2), skip 1 ch, * tr in next ch, ch 2, skip 1 ch, d c in ch just before the tr, skip tr, d c in next st, ch 2, skip 1 ch. Repeat from * around. Join last d c with sl st to 3rd ch of ch-5 first made. **6th rnd:** * S c in next sp, ch 5, s c in next sp, ch 3, skip the 2 d c, s c in next sp, ch 2, 2 d c in same sp, ch 2, s c in same sp, ch 2, d c in same sp, skip tr, d c in next sp, ch 2, s c in same sp, ch 2, 2 d c in same sp, ch 2, s c in same sp, ch 3, skip the 2 d c. Repeat from * around. Join last ch-3 with sl st to base of ch-5 loop first made. Break off. **7th rnd:** Attach thread between 1st and 2nd d c of next scallop, ch 10 (to count as tr and ch-5), * tr at top of next scallop, ch 5, tr at top of next scallop, ch 8, s c in next ch-5 loop, ch 8, tr at top of next scallop, ch 5. Repeat from * around. Join last ch-8 with sl st to 5th st of ch-10 first made.

8th rnd: Sl st to center of ch-5 loop, * ch 5, s c in next loop, repeat from * around, ending rnd with ch-2, d c at base of 1st loop made. **9th rnd:** Ch 12 (to count as tr and ch-7), * tr in next loop, ch 7, tr in same loop, ch 7, tr in next loop, ch 2, skip 1 loop, tr in next loop, ch 7. Repeat from * around. Join last ch-2 to 5th ch of ch-12 first made. **10th rnd:** Sl st in each of next 2 ch, ch 12 (to count as tr and ch-7), * tr in next loop, ch 7, tr in same loop, ch 7, tr in same loop, ch 7, tr in next loop, ch 2, skip ch-2 loop, tr in next loop, ch 7. Repeat from * around. Join last ch-2 to 5th ch of ch-12 first made. **11th rnd:** Sl st in each of next 2 ch, ch 12 (to count as tr and ch-7), * tr in next loop, ch 7, tr in same loop, ch 7, tr in next loop, ch 7, tr in same loop, ch 7, tr in next loop, skip ch-2 loop, tr in next loop, ch 7. Repeat from * around. After last tr is made, join with sl st to 5th ch of ch-12 first made. **12th rnd:** Sl st in each of next 2 ch, ch 12 (to count as tr and ch-7), * tr in next loop (between the 2 tr), ch 7, tr in next loop, ch 7, tr in same loop, ch 7, tr in same loop, ch 7, tr in next loop, ch 7, tr in next loop, ch 2, skip 2 tr, tr in next loop, ch 7. Repeat from * around. Join as usual. **13th rnd:** Sl st in each of next 2 ch, ch 12, * tr in next loop, ch 7, tr in next loop, ch 7, tr in same loop, ch 7, tr in next loop, ch 7, tr in same loop, ch 7, tr in next loop, ch 7, tr in next loop, skip ch-2 loop, tr in next loop, ch 7. Repeat from * around. Join as usual. **14th rnd:** 8 s c in each of next 2 ch-7 loops, * 5 s c in next loop, ch 1; in next loop make 8 d c with ch-1 between d c's, ch 1, 4 s c in next loop, 8 s c in each of next 4 loops. Repeat from * around. **15th rnd:** S c in each of next 12 s c (picking up only the back loop of s c's), * ch 1, ch-4 p, skip 4 s c, d c in next s c, ch 1, ch-4 p, skip 4 s c, d c in next ch-1 sp. In each of next 8 ch-1 sp's make: 1 d c, ch 1, and 1 p. Then ch 1, 1 p, skip 4 s c, d c in next s c, ch 1, 1 p, skip 4 s c, s c in each of next 24 s c. Repeat from * around. Break off.

FOUR SQUARE *Luncheon Set*

Materials: Clark's O.N.T. (4 balls) or J. & P. Coats (3 balls) Mercerized Crochet, size 30, White.

Milward's steel crochet hook No. 11.

2 yds. of white linen, 54 inches wide.

This material is sufficient for a luncheon cloth 52 inches square and 4 napkins, each about 11 inches square. Before starting work, cut linen 54 inches square for cloth, and 4 napkins each 12 inches square. Make a narrow hem all around each napkin and a 1-inch hem around cloth.

Cloth. Starting at one square of corner, ch 54, turn. **1st row:** D c in 6th ch from hook, * ch 2, skip 2 ch, d c in next ch. Repeat from * across (17 sps). Ch 5, turn. **2nd row:** Work 5 sps, 2 bls, 3 sps, 2 bls, 5 sps. Ch 5, turn. Hereafter follow chart, starting from 3rd row (17 rows in square). Break off. Make 4 squares in all. Place a square in each corner of cloth 5 inches in from edge on right side and sew in place.

To make side strips, ch 24, turn and make 7 sps on chain. Ch 5, turn. Work sp over sp back and forth until strip measures same length as distance between 2 squares. Break off. Make 4 strips in all and sew in position over cloth. Cut away linen underneath laces, allowing ¾ inch to make a hem.

Napkin. Ch 30 and work 9 sps. Then continue, following chart. Place over napkin and finish off underneath as for cloth. Fasten and break off.

NAPKIN

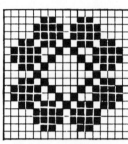

CLOTH

WILD ROSE *Tray Mat*

Materials: Clark's O.N.T. or J. & P. Coats Mercerized Crochet, size 50, 1 ball, White or Ecru.

Milward's steel crochet hook No. 10.

A piece of linen 11 x 17 inches.

When completed, tray mat measures about 12 x 18 inches. Make a narrow hem all around edges and work s c closely around, making a ch-3 p after every inch.

Rose Corners (4): Starting at one end, ch 46, turn. **1st row:** D c in 7th ch from hook, * ch 2, skip 2 ch, d c in next ch. Repeat from * until 14 sps are made. Ch 5, turn. **2nd row:** * Skip ch-2, d c in next d c, ch 2. Repeat from * across. Ch 5, turn. **3rd row:** Make 10 sps, then 2 bls, 1 sp, 1 bl. Ch 12, turn. **4th row:** D c in 4th ch from hook, d c in each of next 8 sts, d c in next d c, ch 2, skip 2 d c, d c in next d c, 4 bls, 9 sps. Ch 5, turn. **5th row:** Sp over sp and bl over bl of previous row. Ch 5, turn. **6th** row: D c in 4th ch from hook, d c in next ch, d c in next d c, 3 bls, 1 sp, 4 bls, 3 sps, 1 bl, 5 sps. Ch 5, turn. **7th row:** 6 sps, 2 bls, 7 sps, 3 bls. Ch 3 turn. Hereafter work in this manner, following diagram. Place corners in place as in illustration. Cut away linen under corners and finish with a narrow hem on wrong side.

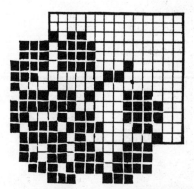

FLOWER WHEEL *Table Cloth*

Materials: Clark's O.N.T. (66 balls) or J. & P. Coats (47 balls) Mercerized Crochet, size 30, White or Ecru.

Milward's steel crochet hook No. 10.

When completed, tablecloth measures about 65 x 80 inches (13 x 16 motifs). Motifs measure about 5 inches in diameter. They are made individually and then sewed together.

Motif. Starting 'at center, ch 9, join with sl st to form ring. **1st rnd:** Ch 3, 23 d c in ring. Join with sl st to 3rd st of ch-3 first made. **2nd rnd:** * Ch 15, s c in each of next 3 d c. Repeat from * around (8 loops). **3rd rnd:** * Work 20 s c in next loop, s c in center s c of 3-s c group. Repeat from * around. Break off. **4th rnd:** Attach thread to 10th s c of next loop, * ch 9, s c in 10th s c of next loop. Repeat from * around. **5th rnd:** Work 10 s c in each loop.

6th to 9th rnds incl: S c in each s c, making 8 increases in each rnd at regular intervals but not directly over those of previous rnd (112 s c in 9th rnd). **10th rnd:** Ch 3, d c in each s c around. **11th rnd:** * Ch 15, skip 4 d c, s c in each of next 3 d c. Repeat from * around. **12th rnd:** Same as 3rd rnd. Break off.

13th rnd: Same as 4th rnd. **14th rnd:** 11 s c in each loop. Join with sl st. **15th rnd:** Ch 6 (to count as d c and ch-3), * d c in same s c, ch 4, skip 4 s c, s c in each of next 3 s c, ch 4, skip 4 s c, d c in next s c, ch 3. Repeat from * around. Join last ch-4 with sl st to 3rd st of ch-6 first made. **16th rnd:** Sl st to center of ch-3 sp, ch 6 (to count as d c and ch-3), * d c in same sp, ch 3, d c in same sp, ch 5, s c in center s c of 3-s c group, ch 4, d c in next ch-3 sp, ch 3. Repeat from * around. Break off. Make 208 Motifs.

To Join Motifs: Place motifs in position (13 x 16 motifs). With over-and-over stitches, sew 2 points of one motif to a corresponding 2 points of the adjacent motif (always having right side of work on top), thus leaving 2 points free on each motif. Then fill in spaces between motifs as follows:

Fill-in-Lace. 1st rnd: Same as 1st rnd of motif. **2nd rnd:** Ch 9, sl st in a ch-3 sp at one point of any one motif, * ch 1, work 10 s c on ch-9, s c in each of next 2 d c of 2nd rnd, ch 9, sl st in a ch-3 sp at next point on same motif, ch 1, work 10 s c on ch-9, s c in each of next 2 d c, ch 9, sl st in a ch-3 sp at next point on next motif, ch 1. Repeat from * around. Break off.

TUDOR
Dinner Cloth

Materials: Clark's O.N.T. (58 balls) or J. & P. Coats (49 balls) Mercerized Crochet, size 20, White or Ecru.

Milward's steel crochet hook No. 11.

When completed, tablecloth measures about 72 x 90 inches (16 x 20 motifs). Motifs measure about 4½ inches in diameter. They are made individually and then sewed together.

Motif. Starting at center, ch 20, join with sl st to form ring. **1st rnd:** Ch 1, 31 s c in ring. Join with sl st. **2nd rnd:** Ch 7 (to count as d tr), make 1 d tr in each of next 3 s c, leaving the last loop of each d tr on hook, * then thread over and work off 2 loops at a time until all loops are worked off; then, ch 12, 1 d tr in each of next 4 s c, leaving the last loop of each d tr on hook. Repeat from * around. Join last ch-12 with sl st to tip of 1st point (8 points in all). **3rd rnd:** Sl st across to center of ch-12 loop, * ch 15, s c in center st of next ch-12 loop. Repeat from * around. **4th rnd:** S c in next loop, ch 4 (to

count as tr), 6 more tr in same loop, * ch 3, 7 tr in same loop, 7 tr in next loop. Repeat from * around. Join with sl st. **5th rnd:** * Ch 8, skip 3 tr, d c in next tr, ch 5, tr in next ch-3 sp, ch 5, tr in same sp, ch 5, skip 3 tr, d c in next tr, ch 5, d c between the two 7-tr groups. Repeat from * around. Join last ch-5 with sl st to base of ch-8 first made. **6th rnd:** * 3 s c in next sp, 2 s c in next sp, ch 5, tr in next sp, ch 5, tr in same sp, ch 5, 2 s c in next sp, 3 s c in next sp. Repeat from * around. Join with sl st and break off. Make 320 motifs.

To Join Motifs. Place motifs in position (16 x 20 motifs). With over-and-over stitches, sew 2 points of 1 motif to corresponding 2 points of the adjacent motif (always having right side of work on top). Then fill in spaces between motifs as follows:

Fill-in-Lace. Work as for 1st and 2nd rnds of motif but, instead of making ch-12 between points, make ch-11 and join the 6th ch of each ch-11 to each joining of motifs and also in center s c of 6-s c groups (which are between points of motifs). Fasten and break off.

135

CENTURY *Luncheon Set*

Materials: Clark's O.N.T. (15 balls) or J. & P. Coats (11 balls) Mercerized Crochet, size 20, White or Ecru.

Milward's steel crochet hook No. 10.

Set consists of 4 place mats, each about 12 x 18 inches, and a center mat about 14 x 24 inches.

Place Mat. Make a chain tightly (about 16 ch sts to 1 inch) to measure about 20 inches, turn. **1st row:** D c in 4th ch from hook, d c in each of next 3 ch, * ch 4, skip 4 ch, d c in each of next 4 ch (1 bl made). Repeat from * across until row measures 17 inches, ending with a bl. (Cut off remaining chain.) Ch. 7, turn. **2nd row:** Skip 2 d c, * tr in last d c of same bl, ch 4, tr in 1st d c of next bl, ch 4. Repeat from * across. Ch 4, turn. **3rd row:** 2 d c in 1st sp, * d c in next tr, ch 4, d c in next tr, 2 d c in sp. Repeat from * across, ending row with a bl. Ch 7, turn.

The last 2 rows constitute the pattern. Repeat these 2 rows until mat measures about 10½ inches deep, ending with a bl-row. Do not break off.

Edging: Ch 4, d c in base of d c just made, * 5 d c in ch-7 sp, d c at tip of next d c, ch 1, d c in base of same d c. Repeat from * around, making 2 d c with ch 3 between the d c's in corner st. Join with sl st. **2nd rnd:** D c in each d c and in each ch-1, making 7 d c in each corner sp. Join with sl st.

3rd rnd: * Ch 3, tr in each of next 2 d c, ch 3, sl st in each of next 4 d c. Repeat from * around, taking care to have a petal come at each corner. Break off. Make 3 more mats.

Center Mat. Make a chain to measure about 26 inches long, turn. Work as for place mat, but having the 1st row measure 23 inches (instead of 17 inches), and working for 12½ inches deep.

LEAF *Luncheon Set*

Materials: Clark's O.N.T. Mercerized Crochet, size 30, 30 balls of Ecru and 10 balls of Sport Green; or J. & P. Coats Mercerized Crochet, size 30, 23 balls of Ecru and 7 balls of Sport Green.

Milward's steel crochet hook No. 11.

This amount is sufficient for 6 place mats, each about 12 x 18 inches and a center mat about 14 x 32 inches. Leaves are made individually and then sewed on.
Gauge: 7 sps make 1 inch; 7 rows make 1 inch.
Place Mat. Starting at one end, with Ecru make a chain tightly to measure about 20 inches, turn.
1st row: D c in 6th ch from hook. * Ch 2, skip 2 ch, d c in next ch. Repeat from * until row mea-

sures 19 inches. Ch 5, turn. Cut off remainder of chain. **2nd row:** Skip ch-2, d c in next d c, * ch 2, d c in next d c. Repeat from * across. Ch 5, turn. Repeat 2nd row until mat measures 12 inches. Break off. Attach Sport Green to one corner and work a row of s c closely together all around edges. Fasten and break off.
Leaf. Starting along center, with Sport Green, ch 45 (to measure about 3 inches), turn. **1st row:** S c in 2nd ch from hook, s c in each ch across. Ch 1, turn. Hereafter always pick up the back loop of each s c of previous row. **2nd row:** S c in each s c across, decreasing 1 s c at both ends (to decrease,

(Continued on page 140)

BROOKSIDE *Luncheon Set*

Materials: Clark's O.N.T. Mercerized Crochet 12 balls of Ecru, size 20 and 6 balls of Dk. Red, size 10; or J. & P. Coats Mercerized Crochet 9 balls of Ecru and 3 balls of Dk. Red.

Milward's steel crochet hook No. 7 or 8.

This material is sufficient for 4 place mats, each about 12 x 18 inches and a center mat about 12 x 24 inches. Corner motifs are made individually and sewed in later.

Gauge: 3 sps made 1 inch; 2 tr-rows and 3 sl st-rows make 1 inch..

Place Mat. Starting at one short end, ch 52 (to measure about 3 inches), turn. **1st row:** S c in 7th ch from hook, sl st in each of next 2 ch, * ch 4, skip 2 ch, sl st in each of next 3 ch. Repeat from * across, ending row with ch 4, s c in last ch (10 loops in all). Ch 4, turn. **2nd row:** Tr in 1st loop, * ch 4, 2 tr in next loop. Repeat from * across. Ch 4, turn.

3rd row: * Skip the tr-group and 1st ch of next ch-4, sl st in each of next 3 ch of same ch-4, ch 4. Repeat from * across. Ch 4, turn. The last two rows constitute the pattern. **4th row:** Same as 2nd row. Ch 4, turn. **5th row:** Same as 3rd row. Turn and break off. **6th row:** Ch 21, 2 tr in last loop of 5th row, * ch 4, 2 tr in next loop. Repeat from * across. Ch 24, turn. **7th row:** Sl st in 7th ch from hook, sl st in each of next 2 ch, ch 4, skip 2 ch, sl st in each of next 3 ch (2 loops made), make 2 more loops on chain, then continue in pattern across, making 4 loops on other chain. Ch 4, turn. **8th row:** Same as 2nd row. **9th, 10th and 11th rows:** Repeat 3rd, 2nd and 3rd rows. Break off at end of 11th row. **12th row:** Work as for 6th row. **13th row:** Work as for 7th row. **14th to 19th rows incl:** Repeat 8th to 13th rows incl. Hereafter work in pattern

(Continued on page 140)

SQUARE-A-DAY
Table Cloth

Materials: Clark's O.N.T. (75 balls) or J. & P. Coats (54 balls) Mercerized Crochet, size 10, White or Ecru.

Milward's steel crochet hook No. 5.

When completed, tablecloth measures amout 70 x 110 inches (3 x 5 blocks). Individual blocks are made, then sewed together.

Block: Starting at center, ch 16, join with sl st to form ring. **1st rnd:** Ch 4 (to count as tr), 4 tr in ring, * ch 7, 5 tr in ring. Repeat from * until 4 groups of tr are made, then ch 7, join with sl st to 4th st of ch-4 first made. **2nd rnd:** Ch 4 (to count

(Continued on page 140)

LEAF *Luncheon Set*

(Continued from page 137)

work off 2 s c as 1 s c). Ch 1, turn. Repeat 2nd row until 16 s c remain. Then continuing with the usual decreases at one end only, increase 2 s c at opposite end every other row, twice. Break off. This completes one half of leaf; for other half, attach thead to foundation chain and work to correspond. Work a row of s c all around leaf. Make 4 leaves for each place mat and sew on as in illustration.
Center Mat. Work as for Place Mats but having the 1st row measure about 32 inches. Then work for 14 inches. Break off. Make 8 leaves and sew on as in illustration.

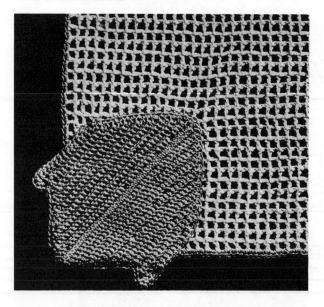

SQUARE-A-DAY *Table Cloth*

(Continued from page 139)

as tr), tr in each of next 4 tr, * 4 tr in corner sp, ch 7, 4 tr in same corner sp, tr in each of next 5 tr. Repeat from * around. Join with sl st as before.
3rd rnd: Ch 7 (to count as tr and ch-3), * skip 3 tr, tr in next tr, ch 3, tr in last tr of tr-group, ch 3, tr in corner st of ch-7, ch 7, tr in same corner st, ch 3, tr in 1st tr of tr-group on other side, ch 3, skip 3 tr, tr in next tr, ch 3. Repeat from * around. Join with sl st in 4th st of ch-7 first made.

4th rnd: Ch 7, * skip ch-3, tr in next tr, ch 3, skip ch-3, tr in next tr, 3 tr in sp, tr in next tr, 4 tr in corner sp, ch 7, 4 tr in same corner sp, tr in next tr, 3 tr in next sp, tr in next tr, ch 3, skip ch-3, tr in next tr, ch 3. Repeat from * around. Join with sl st to 4th st of ch-7 first made. **5th rnd:** Ch 7, * skip ch-3, tr in next tr, 3 tr in sp, tr in each tr of tr-group, 4 tr in corner sp, ch 7, 4 tr in same corner sp, tr in next tr, tr in each tr of tr-group, 3 tr in sp, tr in next tr, ch 3. Repeat from * around. Join with sl st as before. **6th to 20th rnds incl:** Work

in this manner following chart, making ch 3 for sps and ch 7 for each corner sp, and joining each rnd with a sl st. The dotted line on chart shows where each rnd begins. At end of 20th rnd, join and break off. Make 15 blocks in all and sew together on wrong side with over-and-over stitches (3 x 5 blocks).
Edging: 1st rnd: Attach thread to one tr, ch 4 and work tr in each tr and 3 tr in each sp all around. At corners, make 4 tr, ch 7, 4 tr. Join with sl st.
2nd and 3rd rnds: Ch 4, tr in each tr around, making 4 tr, ch 7, 4 tr in each corner. Join and break off.

BROOKSIDE *Luncheon Set*

(Continued from page 138)

straight with no more shapings for 10 more inches, ending with a tr-row. Ch 2, turn. **Next row:** Work in pattern as before but make ch-2 loops across 1st 4 tr-groups and last 4 tr-groups. Turn and break off. **Following row:** Skip the 1st 4 ch-2 loops, attach thread to 5th loop, ch 4, tr in same loop, ch 4, and continue pattern across to within 4 ch-2 loops from end. Hereafter work in pattern to correspond with opposite end. Break off.

Corner Motif: With Dk. Red, ch 34, turn. **1st row:** S c in 2nd ch from hook, s c in each of next 14 ch, skip 2 ch (to form inner corner), s c in each of next 16 ch. Ch 1, turn. Hereafter pick up only the back loop of each s c of previous row. **2nd row:** S c in each s c to within 1 s c from inner corner s c, then skip 1 s c, s c in corner s c, skip 1 s c, s c in each of remaining s c. Ch 1, turn. Repeat 2nd row until 3 s c remain in the row. Then ch 1, sl st in last st. Break off. Make 12 motifs in all. Place them in position, as in illustration and sew with over-and-over stitches, using Ecru thread.

Center Mat. Work exactly as for Place Mat, but making the center section 16 inches long (instead of 10 inches).

A CATALOGUE OF SELECTED DOVER BOOKS
IN ALL FIELDS OF INTEREST

AMERICA'S OLD MASTERS, James T. Flexner. Four men emerged unexpectedly from provincial 18th century America to leadership in European art: Benjamin West, J. S. Copley, C. R. Peale, Gilbert Stuart. Brilliant coverage of lives and contributions. Revised, 1967 edition. 69 plates. 365pp. of text.

21806-6 Paperbound $3.00

FIRST FLOWERS OF OUR WILDERNESS: AMERICAN PAINTING, THE COLONIAL PERIOD, James T. Flexner. Painters, and regional painting traditions from earliest Colonial times up to the emergence of Copley, West and Peale Sr., Foster, Gustavus Hesselius, Feke, John Smibert and many anonymous painters in the primitive manner. Engaging presentation, with 162 illustrations. xxii + 368pp.

22180-6 Paperbound $3.50

THE LIGHT OF DISTANT SKIES: AMERICAN PAINTING, 1760-1835, James T. Flexner. The great generation of early American painters goes to Europe to learn and to teach: West, Copley, Gilbert Stuart and others. Allston, Trumbull, Morse; also contemporary American painters—primitives, derivatives, academics—who remained in America. 102 illustrations. xiii + 306pp.   22179-2 Paperbound $3.50

A HISTORY OF THE RISE AND PROGRESS OF THE ARTS OF DESIGN IN THE UNITED STATES, William Dunlap. Much the richest mine of information on early American painters, sculptors, architects, engravers, miniaturists, etc. The only source of information for scores of artists, the major primary source for many others. Unabridged reprint of rare original 1834 edition, with new introduction by James T. Flexner, and 394 new illustrations. Edited by Rita Weiss. 6⅝ x 9⅝.

21695-0, 21696-9, 21697-7 Three volumes, Paperbound $15.00

EPOCHS OF CHINESE AND JAPANESE ART, Ernest F. Fenollosa. From primitive Chinese art to the 20th century, thorough history, explanation of every important art period and form, including Japanese woodcuts; main stress on China and Japan, but Tibet, Korea also included. Still unexcelled for its detailed, rich coverage of cultural background, aesthetic elements, diffusion studies, particularly of the historical period. 2nd, 1913 edition. 242 illustrations. lii + 439pp. of text.

20364-6, 20365-4 Two volumes, Paperbound $6.00

THE GENTLE ART OF MAKING ENEMIES, James A. M. Whistler. Greatest wit of his day deflates Oscar Wilde, Ruskin, Swinburne; strikes back at inane critics, exhibitions, art journalism; aesthetics of impressionist revolution in most striking form. Highly readable classic by great painter. Reproduction of edition designed by Whistler. Introduction by Alfred Werner. xxxvi + 334pp.

21875-9 Paperbound $3.00

VISUAL ILLUSIONS: THEIR CAUSES, CHARACTERISTICS, AND APPLICATIONS, Matthew Luckiesh. Thorough description and discussion of optical illusion, geometric and perspective, particularly; size and shape distortions, illusions of color, of motion; natural illusions; use of illusion in art and magic, industry, etc. Most useful today with op art, also for classical art. Scores of effects illustrated. Introduction by William H. Ittleson. 100 illustrations. xxi + 252pp.
21530-X Paperbound $2.00

A HANDBOOK OF ANATOMY FOR ART STUDENTS, Arthur Thomson. Thorough, virtually exhaustive coverage of skeletal structure, musculature, etc. Full text, supplemented by anatomical diagrams and drawings and by photographs of undraped figures. Unique in its comparison of male and female forms, pointing out differences of contour, texture, form. 211 figures, 40 drawings, 86 photographs. xx + 459pp. 5⅜ x 8⅜.
21163-0 Paperbound $3.50

150 MASTERPIECES OF DRAWING, Selected by Anthony Toney. Full page reproductions of drawings from the early 16th to the end of the 18th century, all beautifully reproduced: Rembrandt, Michelangelo, Dürer, Fragonard, Urs, Graf, Wouwerman, many others. First-rate browsing book, model book for artists. xviii + 150pp. 8⅜ x 11¼.
21032-4 Paperbound $2.50

THE LATER WORK OF AUBREY BEARDSLEY, Aubrey Beardsley. Exotic, erotic, ironic masterpieces in full maturity: Comedy Ballet, Venus and Tannhauser, Pierrot, Lysistrata, Rape of the Lock, Savoy material, Ali Baba, Volpone, etc. This material revolutionized the art world, and is still powerful, fresh, brilliant. With *The Early Work*, all Beardsley's finest work. 174 plates, 2 in color. xiv + 176pp. 8⅛ x 11.
21817-1 Paperbound $3.75

DRAWINGS OF REMBRANDT, Rembrandt van Rijn. Complete reproduction of fabulously rare edition by Lippmann and Hofstede de Groot, completely reedited, updated, improved by Prof. Seymour Slive, Fogg Museum. Portraits, Biblical sketches, landscapes, Oriental types, nudes, episodes from classical mythology—All Rembrandt's fertile genius. Also selection of drawings by his pupils and followers. "Stunning volumes," *Saturday Review*. 550 illustrations. lxxviii + 552pp. 9⅛ x 12¼.
21485-0, 21486-9 Two volumes, Paperbound $10.00

THE DISASTERS OF WAR, Francisco Goya. One of the masterpieces of Western civilization—83 etchings that record Goya's shattering, bitter reaction to the Napoleonic war that swept through Spain after the insurrection of 1808 and to war in general. Reprint of the first edition, with three additional plates from Boston's Museum of Fine Arts. All plates facsimile size. Introduction by Philip Hofer, Fogg Museum. v + 97pp. 9⅜ x 8¼.
21872-4 Paperbound $2.50

GRAPHIC WORKS OF ODILON REDON. Largest collection of Redon's graphic works ever assembled: 172 lithographs, 28 etchings and engravings, 9 drawings. These include some of his most famous works. All the plates from *Odilon Redon: oeuvre graphique complet,* plus additional plates. New introduction and caption translations by Alfred Werner. 209 illustrations. xxvii + 209pp. 9⅛ x 12¼.
21966-8 Paperbound $4.50

DESIGN BY ACCIDENT; A BOOK OF "ACCIDENTAL EFFECTS" FOR ARTISTS AND DESIGNERS, James F. O'Brien. Create your own unique, striking, imaginative effects by "controlled accident" interaction of materials: paints and lacquers, oil and water based paints, splatter, crackling materials, shatter, similar items. Everything you do will be different; first book on this limitless art, so useful to both fine artist and commercial artist. Full instructions. 192 plates showing "accidents," 8 in color. viii + 215pp. 8⅜ x 11¼. 21942-9 Paperbound $3.75

THE BOOK OF SIGNS, Rudolf Koch. Famed German type designer draws 493 beautiful symbols: religious, mystical, alchemical, imperial, property marks, runes, etc. Remarkable fusion of traditional and modern. Good for suggestions of timelessness, smartness, modernity. Text. vi + 104pp. 6⅛ x 9¼.
20162-7 Paperbound $1.50

HISTORY OF INDIAN AND INDONESIAN ART, Ananda K. Coomaraswamy. An unabridged republication of one of the finest books by a great scholar in Eastern art. Rich in descriptive material, history, social backgrounds; Sunga reliefs, Rajput paintings, Gupta temples, Burmese frescoes, textiles, jewelry, sculpture, etc. 400 photos. viii + 423pp. 6⅜ x 9¾. 21436-2 Paperbound $5.00

PRIMITIVE ART, Franz Boas. America's foremost anthropologist surveys textiles, ceramics, woodcarving, basketry, metalwork, etc.; patterns, technology, creation of symbols, style origins. All areas of world, but very full on Northwest Coast Indians. More than 350 illustrations of baskets, boxes, totem poles, weapons, etc. 378 pp.
20025-6 Paperbound $3.00

THE GENTLEMAN AND CABINET MAKER'S DIRECTOR, Thomas Chippendale. Full reprint (third edition, 1762) of most influential furniture book of all time, by master cabinetmaker. 200 plates, illustrating chairs, sofas, mirrors, tables, cabinets, plus 24 photographs of surviving pieces. Biographical introduction by N. Bienenstock. vi + 249pp. 9⅞ x 12¾. 21601-2 Paperbound $5.00

AMERICAN ANTIQUE FURNITURE, Edgar G. Miller, Jr. The basic coverage of all American furniture before 1840. Individual chapters cover type of furniture—clocks, tables, sideboards, etc.—chronologically, with inexhaustible wealth of data. More than 2100 photographs, all identified, commented on. Essential to all early American collectors. Introduction by H. E. Keyes. vi + 1106pp. 7⅞ x 10¾.
21599-7, 21600-4 Two volumes, Paperbound $11.00

PENNSYLVANIA DUTCH AMERICAN FOLK ART, Henry J. Kauffman. 279 photos, 28 drawings of tulipware, Fraktur script, painted tinware, toys, flowered furniture, quilts, samplers, hex signs, house interiors, etc. Full descriptive text. Excellent for tourist, rewarding for designer, collector. Map. 146pp. 7⅞ x 10¾.
21205-X Paperbound $3.00

EARLY NEW ENGLAND GRAVESTONE RUBBINGS, Edmund V. Gillon, Jr. 43 photographs, 226 carefully reproduced rubbings show heavily symbolic, sometimes macabre early gravestones, up to early 19th century. Remarkable early American primitive art, occasionally strikingly beautiful; always powerful. Text. xxvi + 207pp. 8⅜ x 11¼. 21380-3 Paperbound $4.00

ALPHABETS AND ORNAMENTS, Ernst Lehner. Well-known pictorial source for decorative alphabets, script examples, cartouches, frames, decorative title pages, calligraphic initials, borders, similar material. 14th to 19th century, mostly European. Useful in almost any graphic arts designing, varied styles. 750 illustrations. 256pp. 7 x 10.   21905-4 Paperbound $4.00

PAINTING: A CREATIVE APPROACH, Norman Colquhoun. For the beginner simple guide provides an instructive approach to painting: major stumbling blocks for beginner; overcoming them, technical points; paints and pigments; oil painting; watercolor and other media and color. New section on "plastic" paints. Glossary. Formerly *Paint Your Own Pictures*. 221pp.   22000-1 Paperbound $1.75

THE ENJOYMENT AND USE OF COLOR, Walter Sargent. Explanation of the relations between colors themselves and between colors in nature and art, including hundreds of little-known facts about color values, intensities, effects of high and low illumination, complementary colors. Many practical hints for painters, references to great masters. 7 color plates, 29 illustrations. x + 274pp.
20944-X Paperbound $3.00

THE NOTEBOOKS OF LEONARDO DA VINCI, compiled and edited by Jean Paul Richter. 1566 extracts from original manuscripts reveal the full range of Leonardo's versatile genius: all his writings on painting, sculpture, architecture, anatomy, astronomy, geography, topography, physiology, mining, music, etc., in both Italian and English, with 186 plates of manuscript pages and more than 500 additional drawings. Includes studies for the Last Supper, the lost Sforza monument, and other works. Total of xlvii + 866pp. 7⅞ x 10¾.
22572-0, 22573-9 Two volumes, Paperbound $12.00

MONTGOMERY WARD CATALOGUE OF 1895. Tea gowns, yards of flannel and pillow-case lace, stereoscopes, books of gospel hymns, the New Improved Singer Sewing Machine, side saddles, milk skimmers, straight-edged razors, high-button shoes, spittoons, and on and on . . . listing some 25,000 items, practically all illustrated. Essential to the shoppers of the 1890's, it is our truest record of the spirit of the period. Unaltered reprint of Issue No. 57, Spring and Summer 1895. Introduction by Boris Emmet. Innumerable illustrations. xiii + 624pp. 8½ x 11⅝.
22377-9 Paperbound $8.50

THE CRYSTAL PALACE EXHIBITION ILLUSTRATED CATALOGUE (LONDON, 1851). One of the wonders of the modern world—the Crystal Palace Exhibition in which all the nations of the civilized world exhibited their achievements in the arts and sciences—presented in an equally important illustrated catalogue. More than 1700 items pictured with accompanying text—ceramics, textiles, cast-iron work, carpets, pianos, sleds, razors, wall-papers, billiard tables, beehives, silverware and hundreds of other artifacts—represent the focal point of Victorian culture in the Western World. Probably the largest collection of Victorian decorative art ever assembled— indispensable for antiquarians and designers. Unabridged republication of the Art-Journal Catalogue of the Great Exhibition of 1851, with all terminal essays. New introduction by John Gloag, F.S.A. xxxiv + 426pp. 9 x 12.
22503-8 Paperbound $5.00

A HISTORY OF COSTUME, Carl Köhler. Definitive history, based on surviving pieces of clothing primarily, and paintings, statues, etc. secondarily. Highly readable text, supplemented by 594 illustrations of costumes of the ancient Mediterranean peoples, Greece and Rome, the Teutonic prehistoric period; costumes of the Middle Ages, Renaissance, Baroque, 18th and 19th centuries. Clear, measured patterns are provided for many clothing articles. Approach is practical throughout. Enlarged by Emma von Sichart. 464pp. 21030-8 Paperbound $3.50

ORIENTAL RUGS, ANTIQUE AND MODERN, Walter A. Hawley. A complete and authoritative treatise on the Oriental rug—where they are made, by whom and how, designs and symbols, characteristics in detail of the six major groups, how to distinguish them and how to buy them. Detailed technical data is provided on periods, weaves, warps, wefts, textures, sides, ends and knots, although no technical background is required for an understanding. 11 color plates, 80 halftones, 4 maps. vi + 320pp. 6⅛ x 9⅛. 22366-3 Paperbound $5.00

TEN BOOKS ON ARCHITECTURE, Vitruvius. By any standards the most important book on architecture ever written. Early Roman discussion of aesthetics of building, construction methods, orders, sites, and every other aspect of architecture has inspired, instructed architecture for about 2,000 years. Stands behind Palladio, Michelangelo, Bramante, Wren, countless others. Definitive Morris H. Morgan translation. 68 illustrations. xii + 331pp. 20645-9 Paperbound $3.00

THE FOUR BOOKS OF ARCHITECTURE, Andrea Palladio. Translated into every major Western European language in the two centuries following its publication in 1570, this has been one of the most influential books in the history of architecture. Complete reprint of the 1738 Isaac Ware edition. New introduction by Adolf Placzek, Columbia Univ. 216 plates. xxii + 110pp. of text. 9½ x 12¾. 21308-0 Clothbound $12.50

STICKS AND STONES: A STUDY OF AMERICAN ARCHITECTURE AND CIVILIZATION, Lewis Mumford.One of the great classics of American cultural history. American architecture from the medieval-inspired earliest forms to the early 20th century; evolution of structure and style, and reciprocal influences on environment. 21 photographic illustrations. 238pp. 20202-X Paperbound $2.00

THE AMERICAN BUILDER'S COMPANION, Asher Benjamin. The most widely used early 19th century architectural style and source book, for colonial up into Greek Revival periods. Extensive development of geometry of carpentering, construction of sashes, frames, doors, stairs; plans and elevations of domestic and other buildings. Hundreds of thousands of houses were built according to this book, now invaluable to historians, architects, restorers, etc. 1827 edition. 59 plates. 114pp. 7⅞ x 10¾. 22236-5 Paperbound $4.00

DUTCH HOUSES IN THE HUDSON VALLEY BEFORE 1776, Helen Wilkinson Reynolds. The standard survey of the Dutch colonial house and outbuildings, with constructional features, decoration, and local history associated with individual homesteads. Introduction by Franklin D. Roosevelt. Map. 150 illustrations. 469pp. 6⅝ x 9¼. 21469-9 Paperbound $5.00

MATHEMATICAL PUZZLES FOR BEGINNERS AND ENTHUSIASTS, Geoffrey Mott-Smith. 189 puzzles from easy to difficult—involving arithmetic, logic, algebra, properties of digits, probability, etc.—for enjoyment and mental stimulus. Explanation of mathematical principles behind the puzzles. 135 illustrations. viii + 248pp.
20198-8 Paperbound $2.00

PAPER FOLDING FOR BEGINNERS, William D. Murray and Francis J. Rigney. Easiest book on the market, clearest instructions on making interesting, beautiful origami. Sail boats, cups, roosters, frogs that move legs, bonbon boxes, standing birds, etc. 40 projects; more than 275 diagrams and photographs. 94pp.
20713-7 Paperbound $1.00

TRICKS AND GAMES ON THE POOL TABLE, Fred Herrmann. 79 tricks and games— some solitaires, some for two or more players, some competitive games—to entertain you between formal games. Mystifying shots and throws, unusual caroms, tricks involving such props as cork, coins, a hat, etc. Formerly *Fun on the Pool Table.* 77 figures. 95pp.
21814-7 Paperbound $1.25

HAND SHADOWS TO BE THROWN UPON THE WALL: A SERIES OF NOVEL AND AMUSING FIGURES FORMED BY THE HAND, Henry Bursill. Delightful picturebook from great-grandfather's day shows how to make 18 different hand shadows: a bird that flies, duck that quacks, dog that wags his tail, camel, goose, deer, boy, turtle, etc. Only book of its sort. vi + 33pp. 6½ x 9¼. 21779-5 Paperbound $1.00

WHITTLING AND WOODCARVING, E. J. Tangerman. 18th printing of best book on market. "If you can cut a potato you can carve" toys and puzzles, chains, chessmen, caricatures, masks, frames, woodcut blocks, surface patterns, much more. Information on tools, woods, techniques. Also goes into serious wood sculpture from Middle Ages to present, East and West. 464 photos, figures. x + 293pp.
20965-2 Paperbound $2.50

HISTORY OF PHILOSOPHY, Julián Marias. Possibly the clearest, most easily followed, best planned, most useful one-volume history of philosophy on the market; neither skimpy nor overfull. Full details on system of every major philosopher and dozens of less important thinkers from pre-Socratics up to Existentialism and later. Strong on many European figures usually omitted. Has gone through dozens of editions in Europe. 1966 edition, translated by Stanley Appelbaum and Clarence Strowbridge. xviii + 505pp. 21739-6 Paperbound $3.50

YOGA: A SCIENTIFIC EVALUATION, Kovoor T. Behanan. Scientific but non-technical study of physiological results of yoga exercises; done under auspices of Yale U. Relations to Indian thought, to psychoanalysis, etc. 16 photos. xxiii + 270pp.
20505-3 Paperbound $2.50

Prices subject to change without notice.
Available at your book dealer or write for free catalogue to Dept. GI, Dover Publications, Inc., 180 Varick St., N. Y., N. Y. 10014. Dover publishes more than 150 books each year on science, elementary and advanced mathematics, biology, music, art, literary history, social sciences and other areas.